J·E·S·U·S

THEN AND NOW

J·E·S·U·S

THEN AND NOW

DAVID WATSON
AND SIMON JENKINS

A LION BOOK
Tring · Batavia · Sydney

in association with
Lella Productions

Copyright © 1983 Lion Publishing plc

Published in association with Lella Productions by

Lion Publishing plc
Icknield Way, Tring, Herts, England
ISBN 0 7459 1318 0
Lion Publishing Corporation
1705 Hubbard Avenue, Batavia, Illinois 60510, USA
ISBN 0 7459 1318 0
Albatross Books Pty Ltd
PO Box 320, Sutherland, NSW 2232, Australia
ISBN 0 86760 878 1

First edition 1983 in association with Lella Productions
Reprinted 1983 (twice)
This edition 1987

Printed and bound in Yugoslavia

Introduction

HIS ACTIVE WORK lasted for less than three years. He held no position in public life. He had almost no money and few possessions. He never wrote a book. He never used force. He was hated by the authorities, arrested, condemned, tortured and executed. And yet . . .

His teaching was, and is, of enormous relevance. If true, we have profound answers to the greatest questions that have taxed philosophers down the centuries: issues of life and death, God and humanity.

His character summed up what all of us would most like to be in our best moments. His death, beyond any question of dispute, was the most famous death in human history. No other death has aroused a fraction of such intense feeling over so many hundreds of years. His resurrection was either the most outstanding event of all time, or else a monstrous hoax. And today, nearly 2,000 years afterwards, over 1,400 million people throughout the world profess to follow him: about a third of the world's population.

Few can be passive about Jesus. No other human being has been so loved and so hated, so adored and so despised, so proclaimed and so opposed.

In our present world, two facts seem to be obvious. First, there is increasing interest in the person of Jesus. In the 1960s the common cry seemed to be: 'Glory to man the highest, For man is the master of things.' But if man is the master of things, he is certainly not the master of himself. It is tragically easier to fly to the moon than it is to make peace on the earth. Through staggering scientific and technological advances (which can eliminate us all many times over) we have discovered the bankruptcy of materialism. Human hearts are still crying out for meaning, love, forgiveness, freedom, peace, reconciliation, hope and God. If nothing else, Jesus is supremely relevant to all these basic needs.

Second, in spite of the Bible repeatedly being the world's top bestseller, there is widespread ignorance of the facts about Jesus. When it comes to the significance of his claims, the content of his teaching, the purpose of his death, the evidence for his resurrection or the hope of his return, there is much confusion. Yet, if the records about Jesus are true, then unquestionably there is no greater truth to be found anywhere in the universe.

For these two reasons alone, apart from many others, I was delighted to have a part in the making of the series of video programmes and of this book that goes with them. Not only has Jesus changed the entire course of my life, in ways I could not possibly have imagined when I first came to know him at the age of twenty-one, but also I have become increasingly convinced over the years of the integrity of the evidence surrounding him.

For me, there could be no greater good news in the world. And, in the hostile uncertainties of today, it is surely worthwhile investigating that good news for oneself. *Jesus Then and Now* is designed for that purpose.

David Watson

Contents

'Jesus Then and Now' on video

This book is based on a series of twelve video programmes with the same title. They were produced in response to two developments. The first involves the growth of home video, outstripping even the most optimistic predictions, allowing the television user to plan his own viewing. A parallel development has taken place in the church. Today, many churches encourage people to use their homes for study and fellowship. *Jesus Then and Now* was designed to provide such home-based groups with the facts about Jesus in a video presentation. By bringing the church and video together, *Jesus Then and Now* pioneers new territory in Christian communication.

In late 1980 James Jones told me of his idea for a series of video programmes on the life of Jesus. It was his real faith and enthusiasm for the project at the very beginning that started the ball rolling. Charles Cordle, of Lella Productions, had already grasped the potential of this venture and had set about funding the series through the Trinity Trust.

The basic idea was to produce twelve programmes of broadcast quality that would communicate visually the centre of the Christian faith: Jesus Christ himself. The programmes would explore Jesus not merely as an historical character, but also as a living person, experienced by people today. To do this, scenes from Jesus' life would be dramatized, interviews would take place with Christians from different backgrounds and traditions, and music, dance and film sequences would also contribute.

In these many different ways, television is able to make a subject live. The book is then able to develop some of the themes of the video series in greater depth and to provide the reader with a permanent written record of all that the video programmes dealt with.

I would like to express my sincere thanks to David Watson for his considerable contribution and encouragement throughout, and to Simon Jenkins for his skilful and innovative script-writing. Tina Heath's support was equally important to the series; she introduced the programmes and asked the sort of questions about Jesus that many people would like to ask. The project benefitted greatly from Tim Dean's thoroughness in co-ordinating and guiding the research – and also from the research and production assistance of Olave Snelling. Thanks are also due to our advisors, who clarified our thinking, and helped us pay attention to the theological nuts and bolts of the series. Their names, along with the many others involved in the programmes, are listed elsewhere. To them and to the whole team my gratitude is unbounded. It is my hope that the work of all these people will have the result we have all hoped and prayed for: that twentieth-century audiences will hear and understand the good news of Jesus Christ, and come to know him for themselves.

Tony Tew, *Series Producer*

1
BEGINNINGS

Why look at Jesus?

Jesus Christ grew up in a small, unimportant village nearly 2,000 years ago. He lived for about thirty years before being put to death as a criminal. Why should we, all these centuries later, want to examine the life of this man who lived in such a different age from our own?

The influence of Jesus
Jesus Christ has had an astonishing impact on the world. It is safe to say that no other person has had such an influence on history. In many different parts of the world the influence of Jesus can still be seen in everyday life.

The legal systems of the Western world, for example, have their basis in Christian values. Jesus' teaching and his concern for the poor and the sick have resulted in the social services, hospital work and the care of the dying. The schools, colleges and universities of many countries have their roots in the work of Christians who first taught ordinary people to read and write.

Jesus' influence is still with us, then. It is still important to look for ourselves at the man who has changed so much in our world.

Matters of life and death
Although Jesus lived so long ago, many of the subjects he tackled in his teaching are of timeless importance, still live issues in today's world. He spoke about the dangers of violence, about responsibility towards the poor, about paying taxes. People wanted guidance on these issues in Jesus' time, and they still do today.

On a deeper level, people have been asking questions about the meaning of life and death for thousands of years, although today many people have come to the conclusion that there is no meaning to be found. Jesus spoke clearly and directly about such troubling questions: 'Does life have meaning?' 'Does anything happen after death?' His answers met the needs of people in his time, and many in the twentieth century have found meaning for life in his teaching.

Who Jesus said he was
Another good reason for looking at Jesus is that he made a remarkable impression on the people who knew him well. They came to believe that he was the light of the world, the only way a person could come to God. The way Jesus spoke about himself gave them a reason to believe these things.

If someone were to make such claims about himself today, we

might write him off as deluded, or even mad. But when we look at the way Jesus lived, how he cared for people and provided for their needs, he seems more sane than any of us.

Because the quality of Jesus' life supports what he said about himself, Christians believe that he was who he claimed to be – the Son of God. But whatever we believe about Jesus, it is important that we look for ourselves at what he said and did.

Not Jesus again!
Some people might say that after 2,000 years we have heard enough about Jesus. Certainly Jesus has been the subject of controversy and discussion for centuries. And yet he is still something of a mystery figure today. Many are confused about who he was, why he lived and died.

Some schoolchildren were asked, 'Who do you think Jesus was?' One replied, 'He was the one who took from the rich and gave to the poor.' He had mixed him up with Robin Hood. Another was asked, 'What is a Christian?' He answered, 'Aren't they the people who grow their own vegetables?'

So Jesus is by no means properly understood today. To rediscover the life and teaching of this man, it is vital that we go back to the four Gospels.

How can we know about Jesus?

If we are looking into the life of someone who lived almost 2,000 years ago, how can we be sure of what he said and did? Or, a still more basic question: How do we know about the past at all?

THE CONTROVERSIAL JESUS

'Had there been a lunatic asylum in the suburbs of Jerusalem, Jesus Christ would infallibly have been shut up in it at the outset of his public career.'
Havelock Ellis

'Christianity is the highest perfection of humanity.'
Samuel Johnson

'I call Christianity the one great curse, the one enormous and innermost perversion, the one great instinct for revenge, for which no means are too venomous, too underhand, too underground, and too petty—I call it the one immortal blemish of mankind.'
Friedrich Nietzsche

'If Jesus Christ were to come today, people would not even crucify him. They would ask him to dinner, and hear what he had to say, and make fun of it.'
Thomas Carlyle

The four Gospels

Our main sources for knowing about Jesus are four separate written accounts, known as 'Gospels', or stories bringing 'good news'. Why do we need to have *four* separate records of Jesus' life, when surely one would do?

The value of having four Gospels is that they give us four different angles on the life of Jesus. In any kind of accident investigation today, there is a need to collect the different viewpoints of all those who were witnesses, to get a full idea of what took place. These testimonies will be different in the details they record, but basically they will all report the same event and together give a complete picture of it. So, too, the four Gospels give us a full account of Jesus' words, actions and character.

The purpose of the Gospel writers

Each writer puts his own characteristic stamp on the story. Matthew, Mark and Luke are called the 'synoptic' Gospels: presenting the story from a similar point of view. Mark wrote first, perhaps relying on the apostle Peter for his information; his Gospel is vivid and fast-moving. Matthew and Luke used much of Mark's material, arranging it and adding other material from their own special concerns – Matthew to show how Jesus fulfilled Old Testament prophecy, Luke to

answer the questions and doubts of people who seriously wanted to know about Jesus. John's approach is rather different; he selects his material so as to bring out the deeper significance of the coming of Christ.

Yet, they are all concerned to achieve one basic end. John puts his aim in this way:

Jesus did many other miraculous signs in the presence of his disciples, which are not recorded in this book. But these are written that you may believe that Jesus is the Christ, the Son of God, and that by believing you may have life in his name.
John 20: 30, 31

Non-Christian writers

The main sources we have for knowing about Jesus come from the writings of Christians, and especially from the New Testament itself. But did any writers outside the church say anything at all about him?

Obviously the birth, life and death of the founder of what was then merely another Jewish sect did not greatly interest historians and writers in the Roman Empire. Yet several authors of the time refer to Jesus, and two of them, living within a century of Jesus' birth, are of particular interest.

Josephus

Josephus was a cynical Jewish historian who became a member of the Roman civil service. He was no friend of the growing Christian faith, rather the opposite. But in his work entitled *The Antiquities of the Jews*, he records the following information about Jesus:

At this time there was a wise man who was called Jesus. And his conduct was good and he was known to be virtuous. And many people from among the Jews and from the other nations became his disciples. Pilate condemned him to be crucified and to die. And those who became his disciples did not abandon his discipleship. They reported that he had appeared to them three days after his crucifixion and that he was alive.

So here we have a non-Christian writer telling us that Jesus lived, did good, had a following, suffered, died and was reported alive. Josephus had no Christian axe to grind, yet his record agrees substantially with the four Gospels.

Tacitus
Tacitus was a Roman historian who married the daughter of the Governor of Britain. In one of his writings, he mentioned the execution of Jesus at the order of Pontius Pilate. In AD 115 he recorded the persecution of Christians in Rome by the Emperor Nero. This is his account:

Nero ... punished with the utmost refinement of cruelty a

'There might be something interesting going on here. But how do I know it's for me? I'll look into it – from a safe distance.' This is how some people feel when Jesus is mentioned: intrigued, but a bit worried. That is fine. Reading a book commits a person to nothing. But the Gospels hold plenty of interest for a person wanting to understand life today.

class hated for their abominations, who are commonly called Christians. Christus, from whom their name is derived, was executed at the hands of the Procurator Pontius Pilate in the reign of Tiberius.

How we know about Jesus
So through the writings of the first Christians and at least two authors outside the church, we

are able to know about the life and words of Jesus Christ. Our knowledge of Jesus is far from being shaky or uncertain. Critical study of the Gospels has shown that, even though we cannot prove beyond all doubt the truth of every single detail, they contain a reliable core of historical information about Jesus.

Into what kind of world was Jesus born?

Jesus grew up in a particular country with its own language, customs and identity. The more we know of life as it was lived then, the better we will understand Jesus himself. So what was Palestine like in the time of Jesus?

The country of Palestine
The Jewish people had been led into Palestine, then called Canaan, in the time of Moses. They knew it as 'the Promised Land'.

The area of Palestine in the time of Jesus extended 125 miles/200 kilometres from north to south, and 50 miles/80 kilometres from east to west. It took five days to walk from Nazareth to Jerusalem, and transport was by pack animals like donkeys, or wagons pulled by oxen.

There was an astonishing variety of landscape within this

66 A good and spacious land, a land flowing with milk and honey. **99**

small country. Galilee was green and rich, with evergreen woodland and reliable sources of water. It would be hard to imagine a greater contrast to Galilee than the Dead Sea area with its deserts and stifling heat, only 60 miles/96 kilometres to the south. Water supply and storage were vital. Most of the rivers existed only during the rainy season, or when the snow was melting on the mountains. So towns were built around springs or wells, and water for drinking and irrigation was stored in cisterns and reservoirs.

Political boundaries
Palestine was fractured into a number of political areas. Galilee, in the north, was the home of a number of nationalistic groups fiercely hostile to Roman rule. Judea in the time of Jesus was a third-grade province of the Roman Empire, governed by a Roman Procurator. Samaria was an area within the borders of Judea. The Samaritans were descended

THE NEW TESTAMENT MANUSCRIPTS

Our knowledge of the past is almost completely dependent on written records. But in every case from the ancient world, the original manuscripts have perished and we are dependent on later copies. Yet, this need not mean that our sources are unreliable.

In an age of instant communication, we might feel worried about the accuracy of an event reported weeks after it happened. But when looking at ancient manuscripts, we must expect far greater intervals between the event and its written record. The oldest manuscript we have of Caesar's account of the Gallic War was copied 900 years after he wrote it. And yet scholars consider this a reliable and accurate manuscript.

We are far better provided with New Testament sources. There are many existing manuscripts that contain the whole or parts of the New Testament, a large number of which were copied nearer to the time of composition than with Caesar's *Gallic War*. Because of the wealth of the evidence and its early date, scholars have no doubts whatsoever about the basic reliability of the transmission of the New Testament documents.

One of the oldest complete New Testaments in existence is housed in the

British Museum. It was copied out in the fourth-century AD and is known as the Codex Sinaiticus. But there are individual books and fragments of the New Testament that were copied much earlier than the Codex Sinaiticus. A fragment of John's Gospel exists, three-and-a-half inches long, that we know was copied around the year AD130. It was found in Southern Egypt. That means that a copy of John's Gospel was circulating in that region perhaps only forty years after the Gospel was originally written.

When we compare the different manuscripts of the New Testament that still exist, there are a number of variations between them, most of them minor

differences in wording. More of a problem are instances where a whole passage is missing from some manuscripts, or where another passage appears instead.For example, a significant number of manuscripts do not include the ending of Mark's Gospel, given as Mark 16: 9-20 in most Bibles.

We need to put these variations in perspective. There are only two such passages in dispute, and the more frequent variations in isolated verses do not undermine any important teaching in the New Testament. The manuscript evidence for the New Testament is more plentiful than for any other ancient book.

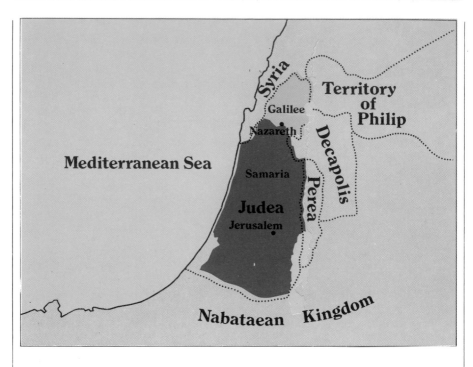

from Jewish stock, but were hated by the Jews of Jesus' time because of religious and political arguments. Surrounding these Jewish areas were a number of other political states, most of which were Gentile.

Roman domination
The overriding fact of political life in Jesus' time was that the Romans were in complete control. This meant that Israel was an occupied territory, paying taxes to a foreign power and with the continual humiliation of the armed forces.

Jesus himself referred several times to the fact of Roman oppression. Once he told his followers:

If someone forces you to go one mile, go with him two miles.
Matthew 5: 41

A Roman soldier could at any time force a Jewish citizen to carry his load for a set distance. Regulations like this stirred up deep resentment among the Jews. They hated Roman rule and all that it meant for their way of life.

The Sadducees
Around the time of Jesus' birth, there were four main religious and political groups in Palestine. One of these groups was known as the Sadducees. The typical Sadducee was an extreme

conservative. He was part of a group made up of the Jerusalem priesthood and wealthy landowners – the aristocracy.

This group had carved out for itself a comfortable working arrangement with the Roman occupiers. Any Sadducee would be extremely unhappy with anyone who threatened this privileged position. The Sadducees were loyal to Caesar and upheld Roman rule.

The Pharisees

A Pharisee was someone who was deeply devoted to the Old Testament Law – the first five books of the Bible. He was determined to apply the whole of

HOW ACCURATE WERE THE GOSPEL WRITERS?

Dr Howard Marshall, a professor of New Testament Studies in the University of Aberdeen, explains why we can be confident about the accuracy of the Gospels:

Many people think that the Gospels are books which only make sense to people who are already Christian believers. They might suggest that the books are written from a biased angle, because they are written by Christians who are trying to convert people, and therefore that you cannot use them as historical documents. But I would say that you can have a purpose in writing a book, and yet write objectively and accurately. If you want to persuade somebody of the truth of something, it is no use telling them a pack of lies that they can instantly see are false.

And so the Gospel writers were not just evangelists trying to convert people. They were trying to make a convincing appeal to historical facts, things that

had really happened. People could ask about them, they could ask people who had been present when Jesus said and did certain things, and find out for themselves that these were true and reliably reported.

It stands to reason we cannot prove that everything in the Gospels happened exactly as it is set down. You just cannot do that with historical reports. What we have to ask is whether there are good grounds for believing that the reports are in general credible. Now take Luke, for example. He begins his Gospel like a history book of the time, with a formal address, stating the sources that he has used, and saying that he has followed things through accurately right from the start. He is therefore claiming to write history—history as good as any other history produced in the ancient world.

Where we can check his information— usually on matters of background,

political situation, geography and so on—we can generally find that he reports a fairly complex situation pretty accurately. It must have taken somebody who was really acquainted with the situation in the ancient world to report it as capably as he did.

The Jews were particularly careful when they were handing down the teaching of their rabbis and their leaders, and there is every reason to think that Christians, living in the same environment, would have the same disciplined way of remembering what Jesus had said, and some of the key stories about him. Facts like these help us to believe that the Gospels are not just stories put together by people trying to invent something interesting or persuasive. They are recording what really did happen in the life of Jesus.

the Law to every part of daily life. As a result, the Pharisees had evolved a system of rules to govern the most minute details of behaviour. For instance, there were thirty-nine types of work prohibited on the Jewish holy day, the Sabbath, and there were regulations to cover the swearing of oaths, the washing of cups and plates, and the maximum travelling distance allowed on holy days.

The Pharisees were a larger group than the Sadducees, numbering about 6,000 in the time of Jesus. They were generally liked by the common people as they too were working men. Their genuine desire was to make the Law bearable for the people, but their zeal for the Law often led them to adopt rigid and harsh attitudes. The typical Pharisee was dissatisfied with Roman rule, but would not normally take part in actively opposing the Romans.

The Zealots

However, a third group, who came to be known as the Zealots after the time of Jesus, *were* active in their opposition to Rome. The Zealots were a set of

Jesus lived in an occupied country. The Romans were in control. Different groups of Jews reacted to their presence in different ways, but most felt the deep resentment of occupied peoples throughout history. Jesus disappointed those who were hoping he would lead a partisan uprising.

loosely organized guerilla groups whose aim was to restore political liberty to God's people.

They believed that the Jews could have no master but God, and therefore allegiance to Caesar was blasphemy. He may often have refused to pay taxes, and conducted terrorist attacks on the Roman forces. His hope was that God would use the freedom fighters to set the

66 **Our God . . . will cause the bright dawn of salvation to rise on us.** 99

Jewish people free – to make Israel an independent nation once more, ruled over by God's Messiah.

Many people in the time of Jesus hoped for the coming of the Messiah. They believed he would be a powerful Jewish king, given special strength by God to restore the fortunes of Israel.

The Essenes
The Essenes were different from the other groups in that they withdrew from normal life. They lived like monks in desert communities, and one such community in the wilderness around the Dead Sea may well have been responsible for writing and copying a large collection of manuscripts known as the Dead Sea Scrolls.

But although the average Essene was removed from the

mainstream of Palestinian society, he too longed for the time when God would intervene in the affairs of the Jewish nation by purifying his people and ridding them of the Romans.

A dangerous area
Some people have said that Jesus was born in a quiet corner of the world where little happened. The truth is far different. Palestine was, and still is, in a highly significant position internationally. It lies across the trading routes of three continents: Europe, Asia and Africa. Politically and religiously it was an extremely unstable area.

The Jewish hope
The Pharisees, the Zealots and the Essenes were united in their expectation that the time was coming when God would act decisively in the nation. This was a hope shared by ordinary working people as well, those who had no allegiance to any of these groups. This hope for the coming of the Messiah was one which the Jewish people had held onto for centuries. It was widely believed that the fulfilment of that hope was near.

The birth of Jesus
In the middle of the conflicting currents of fanatical zeal, political manoeuvring, violence and desperate hope, a young Galilean girl by the name of Mary travelled to Bethlehem, and gave birth to her first son. Luke's account gives us a full

picture of what took place:
In those days Caesar Augustus issued a decree that a census should be taken of the entire Roman world. (This was the first census that took place while Quirinius was governor of Syria.) And everyone went to his own town to register. So Joseph also went up from the town of Nazareth in Galilee to Judea, to Bethlehem the town of David, because he belonged to the house and line of David. He went there to register with Mary, who was pledged to be married to him and was expecting a child. While they were there the time came for the baby to be born, and she gave birth to her firstborn, a son. She wrapped him in strips of cloth and placed him in a manger, because there was no room for them in the inn. Luke 2: 1 – 7

Why was Jesus' birth different?

The New Testament writers regard the birth of Jesus as an extraordinary event in human history, and not just as the birth of another baby. So how do they describe the significance of the birth and humanity of Jesus?

God with us
The New Testament sees Jesus' birth as a marvellous demonstration of God's love for mankind. Christians believe that God the Father sent his Son into the world to live as a human being. Matthew, for example, gives Jesus the name 'Immanuel', which means 'God with us'. God came in the person

66 **They will call him 'Immanuel' – which means, 'God with us'.** **99**

of Jesus to be involved in our world. He came to live among us, to share our joys and sorrows, and ultimately to suffer and die.

This picture of the God who is involved in our world is quite unlike any other picture of God. Many of the Greek philosophers regarded the highest virtue of their gods as apathy – a word that literally means 'freedom from suffering'. These gods had no feelings; they were unconcerned about the world and its suffering. In contrast to that cold image, Jesus was God living in the dirt and pain of human life: the one who had come to rescue us from our suffering.

Jesus the man
The writer of the New Testament letter to the Hebrews says that because Jesus became a human being, he is able to understand us

Jesus was born into a particular place in the world at a particular time in history. His birth in Bethlehem and his life in Galilee are proof that God is not remote from our human lives. He has got involved with us; he knows what life is like.

fully. Jesus knows what it is like to be human. He lived and participated in village life, he built up friendships, did manual labour and knew what it was to laugh and cry.

On a deeper level, the same writer tells us that Jesus is himself a revelation of God; he tells us something about what God is like. And because Jesus was human, we are able to understand God in human terms, terms we can understand. Jesus gives us the best possible picture of God. That picture shows that he loves us, and is prepared to back up his love with action.

Saviour

Luke's account of the birth of Jesus includes the song of Mary, in which she praised God after learning that she was to bear a child. In this song, Mary spoke of God as her Saviour, who would do great things for his people through the child she was carrying:

He has stretched out his mighty arm and scattered the proud with all their plans. He has brought down mighty kings from their thrones, and lifted up the lowly. He has filled the hungry with good things and sent the rich away with empty hands. He has kept the promise he made to our ancestors, and has come to the help of his servant Israel.
Luke 1: 51 – 54

Luke takes the idea of God's involvement in the world one stage further. Jesus came not merely to experience human life, but through his life and death to save God's people from all forms of slavery, to liberate them for a new way of life. He had come on a rescue mission for the sake of all people.

A humble beginning

Many Jews expected the Messiah to come with great splendour and obvious glory. This explains why King Herod was so puzzled that a king should appear in his territory without his hearing of it. Jesus was born in obscurity, not in a palace.

But Jesus had not come to replace King Herod as a political ruler. As his humble birth makes plain, God was not sending Jesus as the king whom the people expected. The Jewish people wanted an inspiring military figure who would recapture Jerusalem and drive out the Romans. But instead Jesus was to point people to the need for obedience and loyalty to God whatever the circumstances.

Throughout his life, Jesus' concern was not so much for the great and powerful, but for the common people of Mary's song: the poor, the hungry, the disadvantaged, the unloved. It was appropriate that he was born in simple surroundings to an un-remarkable couple, and his family were typical of the people for whose sake he had come – ordinary people living ordinary lives.

2
TEMPTATION

Who was John the Baptist?

In all four Gospel accounts, John appears at the very beginning of the story of Jesus' adult life. Matthew's Gospel introduces John the Baptist in these words: *At that time John the Baptist came to the desert of Judea and started preaching. 'Turn away from your sins,' he said, 'because the kingdom of heaven is near!'* So who was John the Baptist? John was related to Jesus: his mother was Mary's cousin. He was the only son of Zechariah and Elizabeth and was born to them in their old age. When John began preaching in the desert, people travelled long distances to hear him. Many of them must have expected him to be the Messiah that they were hoping for.

The kingdom of God

John began his message with the news that the kingdom of God was about to arrive. John saw himself as the one come to announce the coming kingdom. When Jesus began to preach, he began his message in exactly the same way. 'The right time has come,' he said, 'the kingdom of God is near!' So what exactly was the kingdom of God?

A popular expectation

At various times throughout their history, the Jewish people had been the victims of oppression. By Jesus' time, Judea was a small occupied province in the Roman Empire.

WHAT IS THE KINGDOM OF GOD?

Dr Howard Marshall explains: The main theme of the teaching of Jesus was what he called 'the kingdom of God'. What did he mean by this?

● The 'kingship', or rule of God. God was active in the world in order to save people from their sins and their failures, and to establish peace and righteousness.

● God was doing this through Jesus as his agent. So the things Jesus did in his ministry—when he forgave sins, when he made people better from their illnesses—these were the kind of things that were bringing God's rule into effect, instead of the rule of sin, evil and suffering.

● God's rule was coming through what Jesus did, and it will be fully established in the future when Jesus comes again openly and clearly as the Son of God. Then he will establish God's final reign of peace, justice and love.

Despite this history of domination, the Jews believed that God had not abandoned them, but that he would free them as he had done in the exodus. They longed for the time when God would send them his Messiah to establish the kingdom of God on earth. The Messiah was to be a great national figure like King David, who would make Israel an independent kingdom by throwing off the domination of Rome by force. This Messiah would then rule God's kingdom as a warrior-king.

John and God's kingdom

Suddenly, John appeared in the desert like one of the Old Testament prophets, preaching about the coming of God's kingdom. Could it be that John was the expected Messiah? John flatly denied it. He said that he was merely the one who prepared the way for the greater one to follow him – and he pointed to Jesus as that person.

John surprised his Jewish listeners by telling them that they needed to escape coming judgement, rather than prepare for political triumph. It seemed that John's idea of the kingdom of God was quite different from the popular hope of the Jewish people.

Jesus and God's kingdom

The teaching of John and, after

PRACTICAL REPENTANCE

What does repentance mean in practical terms? This was a question Graham Turner had to come to terms with when, as Economics Correspondent for the BBC, he felt a very specific call from God to repent:

Repentance meant very simply in my case doing what God told me to do. I think there are two things. There is remorse, which is feeling sorry, and there is repentance, which means being sorry enough to actually do something about it. In my case that meant doing what God told me to do: to put things right that were wrong in my life.

He told me four things, very simply. One was that I'd had a flirtation with another girl—other than my wife—and he said to me, you tell her about it. Then the second thing was that I had been fiddling on my tax returns, so he told me to go along to the tax man and tell the tax man that I had been fiddling. The third thing was that I had also been fiddling on my expenses—I was working for the BBC at the time. God said to me, 'Go and pay them back a thousand pounds.'

And then, as if that was not enough, the fourth thing he said was, 'You've treated your neighbours like dirt.

You have built an extension on to the garage.' (It was a very simple thing, but it actually cut into their sunlight.) 'Write them a letter and tell them you are very sorry for the way you have treated them.' We had moved from the house by that time.

So in concrete terms that is what repentance meant to me. And it seems to me that unless repentance involves concrete acts, actually putting right the things God tells you to put right, then there is not much meat in the sandwich.

him, of Jesus about the kingdom of God must have disappointed many Jews because it did not include the idea of the nation's political supremacy. In the teaching of Jesus, the kingdom of God was not a territory or a particular race or nation. It was to be the rule of God over the lives of people everywhere, not just among the Jews and not only within the borders of Israel.

Repentance

John appealed to his listeners to do something positive. He told them to repent of their sins. Today, the word 'repent' has old-fashioned and negative overtones. But basically it means an about-turn. We all go through life our way, doing the things we choose to do. But if we are seriously looking for God, we have to be willing to stop going in our own direction, let go of what we know is wrong, turn right round and begin to live as God wants. Repentance sounds negative, but it actually means a positive change in direction. This is exactly what John asked of his listeners.

Today we may think that we are not all that selfish, and do not need to repent. But when we compare the way we live with what God asks of us, we can see that we fall far short. For example, Jesus once said that the greatest commandment was that we should love God with all the strength that we have. No one has kept this standard, no matter how good he may seem. And so

we need to repent and allow God his rightful place at the centre of our lives.

Baptism

To show publicly that they had repented, people were baptized by John. Baptism, as John practised it, was simply an outward sign of inward cleansing from sin. Even today, signs are very important. For example, shaking hands is a useful gesture used in the Western world to symbolize agreement and friendship. The actual friendship

Jesus spent forty days and nights in the wilderness of Judea. In this total isolation, he came face to face with the temptation to find some other way of living than the one God had called him to.

is more important than the symbol, yet shaking hands is important as it helps us to demonstrate that friendship.

So baptism in John's time worked partly in that way. It was a sign that a person had been washed clean from sin. He was making a break with the past and starting a new life with God. The Gospels tell us that while John was preaching and baptizing people in the Jordan, Jesus too came to him for baptism.

Why did Jesus leave Nazareth?

Up until this time, Jesus had grown up in Nazareth, his parents' home town, and had worked as the local carpenter. But suddenly he left all this behind and came to John to be baptized. Why did he do this?

The beginning of a new life
When Jesus heard that John was preaching and baptizing in the River Jordan, he knew that the time had come for him to begin his real work. After being baptized, Jesus began to lead a new way of life as a travelling teacher and healer, telling people the good news of God's kingdom. Clearly Jesus saw his baptism as the first step in the new work God had given him to do.

Why was Jesus baptized?
Matthew tells us about the baptism of Jesus in these words:

At that time Jesus arrived from Galilee and came to John at the Jordan to be baptized by him. But John tried to make him change his mind. 'I ought to be baptized by you,' John said, 'and yet you have come to me!' But
Jesus answered him, 'Let it be so for now. For in this way we shall do all that God requires.' So John agreed. As soon as Jesus was baptized, he came up out of the water. The heaven was opened to him, and he saw the Spirit of God coming down like a dove and alighting on him. Then a voice said from heaven, 'This is my own dear Son, with whom I am pleased.' Matthew 3: 13 17

Why did Jesus insist on undergoing baptism by John? Surely God's Messiah would not need to repent; he would have no sins to give up!

Dedication to God
Jesus persuaded John to baptize him by saying, 'Let it be so for now. For in this way we shall do all that God requires.' Although the exact meaning of this reply is

open to different interpretations, it clearly shows that Jesus saw his baptism as a way of openly dedicating himself to God at the beginning of his three-year ministry. He knew that God wanted him to do this.

Later in his ministry, Jesus sometimes spoke of the suffering and pain in his coming death as a 'baptism'. So by being baptized by John now, he was taking on a way of life that would involve him in a great deal of suffering and pain.

Jesus and the people

Luke's account of the baptism tells us that among the many people coming to John were corrupt soldiers and tax-collectors. Jesus' mission was all about such people – those who recognized that they were in the wrong and were willing to let God do something about it.

Throughout his ministry, Jesus was criticized by his opponents for associating with the outcasts of society. So it was appropriate that he should begin his new life by being seen with them now.

The voice and the dove

At the River Jordan, Jesus was publicly declaring his determination to obey God and to accept his ministry of suffering. In return he received God's encouragement. Jesus saw a dove descending on him, and heard a voice which said 'This is my own dear Son, with whom I am pleased.'

What did all this mean?

God was reassuring Jesus that he would not be alone in facing the struggles of his life. He was pleased with what Jesus had just done, and was openly showing that he would support him. By

> **❝As Jesus was coming up out of the water, he saw . . . the Spirit descending on him like a dove. ❞**

addressing Jesus as 'my Son', God the Father was also telling Jesus something about his future mission. This work was not just something that Jesus had thought up on his own. It was a task that God had called him to do.

Into the desert

It is surprising to read that after all the encouragement Jesus had received at his baptism, immediately after the event he went into the desert and was alone, hungry and tempted.

And yet it is true for many people that after periods of encouragement or success they face doubt and temptation. Where God is at work, evil is also at work, trying to overcome the good. This was true for Jesus. At the beginning of this vital ministry, which was to change the whole of mankind, Jesus faced a tremendous battle. This was more than a struggle to come to terms with the ministry in his own mind: Jesus faced the temptations of the devil.

Does the devil really exist?

Many people would want to stop at this point to ask whether there really is a personal devil. The explosion of science and technology over the last century has meant that, for many, belief in the supernatural has become unpopular. The existence of God, the devil and miracles are just a few of the beliefs that some twentieth-century people have seen as superstitions. Can we reasonably believe in a personal source of evil today?

Horns and a tail?

It is easy to laugh at the medieval idea of the devil with a tail and horns, but the picture we are given in the Bible is very different – and we have to take it more seriously. In the Bible, the devil is a malignant, personal force, behind the scenes of the physical world, who works against the good of humanity.

To say that the discoveries of modern science have shown such an idea to be outdated is wrong. The scientist is concerned with the workings of the physical world, and therefore a non-physical devil is beyond the scope of his research. Modern scientists are also far less confident than they were at the beginning of this century about dismissing the supernatural.

Jesus and the devil

The most convincing evidence for belief in the devil lies in the fact that Jesus took his reality seriously. No other person in the Bible spoke so frequently or

Ouija boards, seances, witchcraft – many occult practices pose as nothing more than a way of relieving the boredom of life. But once a person is drawn in, the dangers become all too real. There seems to be a destructive force of evil lying behind these apparently innocuous activities.

warned his listeners so strongly about the devil and his activities.

Jesus' belief in the devil was of major importance to the way he carried out his mission in the world. He spoke of the devil as an evil prince who ruled the world and used his powers against people. Jesus saw many of his healing miracles as part of the process of driving back his opponent's kingdom. And he spoke of his own death as a final battle to break the devil's rule.

Although Jesus spoke about the devil as a powerful figure, there is no suggestion that he is as powerful as God. Rather, Jesus said that the devil is a creature, with limited power. If we can take Jesus' teaching seriously, we also have to come to terms with his warnings about a literal, personal devil, who lies behind the evil in this world.

The battle

Many writers in the New Testament speak about a great conflict that is taking place between the forces of good under God's command, and the forces of evil under the devil's command. This struggle between good and evil became a part of our world when mankind first rebelled against God. Ever since that time, the world has been like a battlefield on which this conflict is fought.

Jesus was taken into the heat of this battle as he wrestled alone

THE OCCULT TODAY

Over the last twenty or so years in the West, there has been renewed interest in the devil and the occult. Not only are people beginning to believe in the existence of evil beings again, but unfortunately they are also getting involved with them.

C.S. Lewis, a Christian writer, once said, 'There are two equal and opposite errors into which our race can fall about the devil. One is to disbelieve in their existence. The other is to believe, and to feel an excessive and unhealthy interest in them.' We see both these extremes in Western society today.

Doreen Irvine has had firsthand experience of the occult, though now a Christian and involved in Christian work. She was asked whether we can believe in a personal devil in the twentieth century:

'Yes, we certainly can. I know he exists because for many years I served him as a satanist and a witch, and a lot of people today are involved in witchcraft and satanism. But at the same time there are still many people who dismiss Satan as an outmoded nonsense figure from the Dark Ages with a pair of horns and a pitchfork. Some people laugh at you if you speak and warn of a personal devil and demons.

'But the devil, who is the greatest saboteur and the greatest deceiver of all times, would prefer to keep it that way because disbelief in his existence is his best camouflage. The enemy you cannot see and do not know is far more powerful and dangerous than the one you do see and know about.'

with temptation in the desert. It is easy to see why all the evil forces of the devil should now be directed against him. Jesus had come to rescue men and women from their slavery to a sinful way of life. If Jesus himself could be made to sin, then the whole of this rescue attempt would be ruined.

The devil's strategy

Matthew and Luke both tell us that after his baptism Jesus fasted (went without food) for forty days. In this weak condition he faced an onslaught of temptation. Matthew and Luke present these temptations in the form of three specific challenges the devil made to Jesus.

In each temptation, the devil was attempting to divert Jesus from the real purpose of his mission. Jesus had just accepted the task of setting God's people free, but he knew that freedom could only come about through his own suffering and death. These three temptations basically suggested that he did not need to go through such suffering – there was a much easier and more popular way.

Temptation 1: Stones into bread

Jesus, full of the Holy Spirit . . . was led by the Spirit in the desert, where for forty days he was tempted by the devil. He ate nothing during those days, and at the end of them he was hungry. The devil said to him, 'If you are the Son of God, tell this stone to become bread.' Jesus answered, 'It is written: "Man does not live on bread alone."' Luke 4: 1 – 4

Jesus had been in the desert for forty days without eating. So why would it have been wrong for him to provide food for himself by turning stones into bread?

The devil found a way to get at Jesus through his need for food. But his objective was not merely to get Jesus to eat. He wanted Jesus to surrender to an important principle by using his miraculous powers to satisfy his own personal needs. This was something that Jesus consistently refused to do throughout his life. He always used his powers to help other people, as when, on several occasions, Jesus provided food in a similar way for large hungry crowds.

In his reply to the devil, Jesus acknowledged that God is concerned that we should have food to eat. He said, 'Man does not live on bread *alone*.' Bread is important, but it is not the most important consideration. It is more important to live a life of obedience to God.

Temptation 2: Political power

The devil led him up to a high place and showed him in an instant all the kingdoms of the world. And he said to him, 'I will give you all their authority and splendour, for it has been given to me, and I can give it to anyone I want to. So if you worship me, it

will all be yours.' Jesus
answered, 'It is written:
"Worship the Lord your God and
serve him only."' Luke 4: 5 – 8

*The best way to change things has always
seemed to be through political or military
power. The devil tempted Jesus to go that
way. But Jesus knew his kingdom was quite
different, changing people from within
rather than by outward force.*

Many people think of Jesus as a
kind, loving person who did good,
healed the sick, cared for people,
and eventually gave up his life
for us. He does not seem to be a
person who would be tempted to
lust after power. So how was this
a temptation for Jesus?

Although Jesus was good and
kind, that is not the full picture.
The image of 'gentle Jesus, meek
and mild' is inadequate. It does
not take account of Jesus as a
kingly figure who rules in God's
kingdom. To rule over all the

nations was the ultimate aim of his mission, and so the words the devil spoke would have been a powerful temptation for him.

This temptation also held out to Jesus a role that would have earned him great popular support: a political Messiah. This way, Jesus would not have to face the daunting prospect of the cross. If he would only worship the devil, he would become the popular figure the Jewish people were looking for. But Jesus knew that God's good rule would never be brought about by evil methods. To worship the devil would be a complete denial of the kingdom of God.

Temptation 3: A miraculous stunt

The devil led him to Jerusalem and had him stand on the highest point of the temple. 'If you are the Son of God,' he said, 'throw yourself down from here. For it is written: "He will command his angels concerning you to guard you carefully; they will lift you up in their hands, so that you will not strike your foot against a stone."' Jesus answered, 'It says, "Do not put the Lord your God to the test."' Luke 4: 9 – 12

Why should Jesus find it a temptation to leap from a great height? Here again, Jesus was being tempted to attract instant popularity through an astonishing miracle. For the Jews at the time, there was an expectation that the Messiah would dramatically appear in the temple. So this temptation brought these two ideas together as a means of forcing people to recognize Jesus as the Messiah.

The devil backed up his case by quoting from Psalm 91 in the

> 66 **We are not fighting against human beings, but against the wicked spiritual forces.** 99

Old Testament. The devil can use the Bible, but the way in which he uses it is to twist its meaning to make it into a lie. In Psalm 91, the writer says that God cares for the person who trusts and depends on him. But the devil twisted it to suggest that God guarantees to protect us even if we do something foolish or wrong. Jesus pointed out in reply that to do this would be to test God and to take advantage of his love for us.

Other temptations
At the end of his account of the temptations, Luke records, 'When the devil had finished all this tempting, he left him until an opportune time.' Jesus had obviously been tempted in the past, and he would be again in the future. Throughout his life, he faced temptations of all kinds. He was even tempted to give up his mission in the hours before his arrest. He overcame these temptations, but only with the greatest difficulty.

What do Jesus' temptations teach us?

It is encouraging to know that Jesus faced temptation as we all do, and that he was fully human. Even more encouraging is the fact that he did not give way, but overcame his temptations. Jesus knew what it meant to be tempted and yet overcame. As we face the problem of temptation in our lives, we can learn a lot from him.

Temptation is not sinful

Many people feel guilty when they have been tempted about something, even if they have not given in to the temptation. We need to know that temptation in

The last of Jesus' wilderness temptations was to go to Jerusalem and throw himself down from the mighty east wall of the Temple, believing that God would save him from harm. Would people who followed him because of such a miracle really have a clue what he had come to bring to the world?

itself is not wrong. After all, Jesus himself was tempted, but the writers of the New Testament were all convinced that his life was completely free from any kind of sin. What is wrong is when we give way to temptation, or toy around with the ideas temptation gives us.

Resisting temptation

Those who make it a habit to give in to temptation never really know how powerful the temptations are that control them. In fact, it is only when we start to resist temptation that we discover its strength. Driving a car at speed, we may not realize how fast we are travelling until we have to brake in an emergency. Temptation is like that. It is only when we try to say 'no' to our desires that we realize their attraction and force.

We soon discover that by ourselves we cannot resist temptation for long. It is not in our power to keep living in the way that Jesus did. We need outside help, and here the example of Jesus is useful to look at.

Jesus and the Bible

In all his replies to the devil, Jesus quoted from the Old Testament; he did not simply rely on himself. Like any Jewish boy, Jesus had been brought up on the Old Testament and knew its writings inside out. As a result, he was able to recognize the temptations for what they were.

But Jesus not only knew the

We cannot live in this world without being tempted! Jesus himself was tempted. This shows that temptation is not sinful in itself. The sin comes when we harbour temptation and give way.

Bible and committed it to memory. He lived by its teaching. The Bible is not some kind of magical book where we just have to say the right words to have power over the devil. It is as we read and understand the Bible and, more important, as we learn to obey God and live in the way the Bible teaches, that we can use the Bible in defeating temptation.

Temptation strikes when we are weak

The devil is a dirty fighter. We

are especially open to temptation when we are weak, ill or exhausted. This was true of Jesus who had been without food and without human company for some considerable time. The devil tempted him by offering him both food and popularity, an offer that would have greatly appealed to him at a time like that. So we need to be aware that we too will be tempted during times of weakness.

Jesus understands temptation
Jesus knew for himself what it was like to be tempted. One New Testament writer put it like this:

We have a great High Priest who has gone into the very presence of God – Jesus, the Son of God. Our High Priest is not one who cannot feel sympathy for our weaknesses. On the contrary, we have a High Priest who was tempted in every way that we are, but did not sin.
Hebrews 4: 14 – 16

Because he knew the force of temptation, Jesus can sympathise when we are tempted. But he does not sympathise as one wounded soldier to another. He meets us as the one person who has defeated sin by the power of God. So Jesus does more than simply help us face our weakness; he gives us strength to overcome

temptation as he did.

Our relationship with God
By looking at the way Jesus was tempted, we can understand better the devil's strategy. It is significant that the devil opened each temptation by saying to Jesus, '*If* you are the Son of God . . .' He was trying to cast doubts in Jesus' mind that he really was the Son of God.

This is the devil's approach with us as well. He attempts to come between us and God. He can attack us most effectively when our relationship with God is poor. And if we do fall into sin, he tries to prevent us from approaching God for forgiveness by telling us that God no longer loves or cares for us.

The devil, then, consistently attacks our relationship with God, which highlights that

66 God keeps his promise, and he will not allow you to be tested beyond your power to remain firm. 99

relationship as vitally important in the battle to resist temptation. It is only as we rely on God's strength, rather than our own, that we can defeat temptation, as Jesus did.

3
DISCIPLES

Why did Jesus call the disciples?

When we look at the accounts of Jesus' life, we soon become aware of the many mistakes made by his close associates, the disciples. There were times when they completely missed the point of what Jesus was saying, and sometimes Jesus had to repeat and explain his parables because they found them so puzzling.

On one occasion Jesus was exasperated with them: 'Don't you know or understand yet?' he asked. 'Are your minds so dull? You have eyes – can't you see? You have ears – can't you hear?' So why did Jesus need to have disciples around him in the first place?

The call of the disciples

From the early days of his ministry, Jesus began to call individuals to a life of following him. These followers became known as his disciples. Jesus then chose twelve of these disciples, and they formed an inner circle who were to be with him almost constantly throughout his ministry. It seems that his choosing of the twelve was an event that Jesus saw as crucial to the success of his mission. Luke tells us that on the night before the event,

Jesus went up a hill to pray and spent the whole night there praying to God. Luke 6: 12

But why did Jesus call these twelve disciples? Mark's account gives us the answer:

Jesus appointed twelve – designating them apostles – that they might be with him and that he might send them out to preach and to have authority to drive out demons. Mark 3: 14, 15

They were to be in the company of Jesus. They were to be 'sent' to preach (the word 'apostle' literally means 'one who is sent').

They were to be given his authority to expel the powers of evil.

In other words, Jesus was to train them to do his work.

Who were the disciples?

This is Luke's list of the twelve apostles:

When day came, Jesus called his disciples to him and chose twelve

THE TWELVE APOSTLES

Simon Peter was a Galilean fisherman when Jesus called him to be his disciple. Peter was often rash and impetuous in his actions, but his faith in Jesus was strong, and he was the first disciple to recognize Jesus as 'the Messiah, the Son of the living God'. At the Last Supper, Peter boldly declared that he would never desert Jesus but only hours later he denied that he had ever known him. Despite Peter's denial, Jesus met with him after the resurrection and gave him an important role in the early church. It was Peter who preached on the Day of Pentecost when 3,000 joined the church. Peter was also one of the first to realize that the gospel was for all people, and not just the Jews.

Andrew was Peter's brother and was also a fisherman. Originally he was one of John's disciples, but when John declared that Jesus was 'the Lamb of God', Andrew and another disciple began to follow Jesus. Andrew took Simon Peter to meet Jesus.

James was the brother of John. Both of them were fishermen. Jesus nicknamed them 'the sons of thunder' because of their fiery nature. Once, they wanted to call down fire from heaven on a Samaritan village that had turned Jesus away, and they also asked Jesus for the most privileged places in his kingdom. Yet Peter,

James and John formed the group who were closest to Jesus within the company of the disciples. After Jesus' resurrection, James was executed by Herod Agrippa for his faith in Jesus.

John was probably the disciple who was closest of all to Jesus. It seems likely that he referred to himself as 'the disciple whom Jesus loved' in the Gospel bearing his name. Peter and John went together to the empty tomb on the first Easter morning, and John 'saw and believed'. With Peter, John was the leader of the Jerusalem church, and probably wrote the three letters and the vision that bear his name in the New Testament.

Philip was also a Galilean who came from Bethsaida. He is mentioned only a few times in the Gospels, and seems to have been full of questions about who Jesus was and what he had come to do.

Bartholomew may well also have been known as Nathanael, whom Philip introduced to Jesus.

Matthew was a tax-collector who left his lucrative job to follow Jesus. Also known as Levi, he invited Jesus to a feast in his home, where Jesus began to meet with tax-collectors and other despised elements in Jewish society.

Thomas is most famous for his refusal to believe in the

resurrection after Jesus had appeared to the apostles when Thomas was elsewhere. Jesus appeared again, this time to all the apostles. Thomas's confession, 'My Lord and my God', is the climax of John's Gospel.

James, son of Alphaeus, may have been a younger brother to James and John.

Simon the Patriot may well have been attached to a political and religious party known later as the 'Zealots'.

Judas, son of James, was also known as Thaddaeus.

Judas Iscariot always appears last in the list of the disciples called by Jesus, with the description of the one who betrayed Jesus. Judas was the treasurer of the group, and according to John's Gospel used this position to take money from the common fund for his own use. Judas is infamous for betraying Jesus by leading his teacher's enemies to the place where he knew Jesus would be at night. But after betraying Jesus, he was filled with horror and guilt, and committed suicide.

of them, whom he named
apostles: Simon (whom he
named Peter) and his brother
Andrew; James and John, Philip
and Bartholomew, Matthew and
Thomas, James son of Alphaeus,
and Simon (who was called the
Patriot), Judas son of James,
and Judas Iscariot, who became
the traitor. Luke 6: 13 – 16

What were these disciples like?
On the positive side, each of the
twelve gave up his job to follow

*In a parable, Jesus pictured a tower that
was begun but not finished. He taught
that people should not begin to follow him
until they had counted the cost of
discipleship. Otherwise they would make
the Christian way look pointless and
ridiculous.*

Jesus, and although Jesus'
teaching often perplexed them,
they stayed with him. Peter once
said to Jesus, 'We have left
everything to follow you!' Yet the
disciples were often something of
a disappointment to Jesus,
because they were slow to
understand his mission. They
argued about which of them was
the greatest; James and John
once asked Jesus for superior
positions in the kingdom of
heaven; and Peter tried to deter
Jesus from talking about his
death. So the disciples seem to
have been quite ordinary men,
with the normal blend of good
qualities and weaknesses.

Even within this inner circle of
twelve disciples, there were
three who were specially close to
Jesus and shared some of the
important moments of his life.
Peter, James and John were
present at Jesus' transfiguration
in the middle of his ministry, and
also at the end, when he took
them to pray in the Garden of
Gethsemane.

Jewish discipleship
Discipleship was common in the
Jewish society of Jesus' time.
The would-be disciple chose a
spiritual teacher for himself in
order to study his teaching.
These teachers were called
'Rabbis', a word which literally
means 'great one'. The Rabbis
were highly respected in society.
It was said that if an enemy
captured your parents and your
Rabbi, you should pay the
ransom for your Rabbi first!

Jesus himself was addressed as 'Rabbi' on a number of occasions as a mark of respect. So what was it like to be a disciple of this Rabbi Jesus?

Jesus' discipleship

Like the Rabbis of his time, Jesus gave his disciples more than just spoken teaching. They lived with him, they saw him working among the common people and they shared his whole life. He called them to join him in bringing God's good news to other people.

But Jesus' method of choosing and training his disciples departed from the Jewish pattern in at least one important way. Disciples normally attached themselves to the Rabbi of their choice, but Jesus chose the twelve. And there were times when Jesus prevented other people from becoming his followers.

Jesus was not setting out to form a religious club full of people who agreed with each other – quite the reverse. Some members of the group would have been violently opposed to each other before becoming disciples of Jesus. Simon the Zealot, for example, probably belonged to a revolutionary group dedicated to the overthrow of the Roman occupiers by violence. He would hardly have been pleased by Jesus' choice of Matthew as his fellow disciple. Matthew was a tax-collector for the Romans, a collaborator of the worst sort. Yet Jesus saw in

these diverse personalities the qualities that were needed in the church's first leaders.

The importance of the disciples

The twelve disciples played a very important part in the life and work of Jesus. Although one of the group, Judas, betrayed

66 Come with me, and I will teach you to catch men. 99

Jesus, the other disciples remained committed to him and were witnesses to all that he had said and done. Everything that we know about Jesus has come down to us because of their discipleship.

After the death and resurrection of Jesus, the disciples were mobilized by the Holy Spirit to spread the news of who Jesus was and what he had achieved. Without them, the message of Christianity would never have spread in the way it did. They were crucial to all that Jesus had come to do.

Discipleship is vital today

For similar reasons, our discipleship today is crucial to God's work in the world. We can see this by looking at any kind of discipleship. The political, social and religious movements of the twentieth century have all had one thing in common: they have relied on the effort and sacrifice of their followers. If ordinary people are not willing to work for a cause, however great it may seem, then the cause will collapse.

But when even a small group of people become convinced followers of a cause, the effect they can have is enormous. It is said that in the Russian Revolution of October 1917, only one per cent of the Russian people believed in the ideals behind the revolution. And the same was true of the early church, who had an impact far beyond their numbers.

The mission of Jesus Christ in the world today depends on the willingness of ordinary Christians to devote their resources – time, energy, money – to Christ. If the church is weak today, it is because Christians are not prepared to follow Jesus with the same commitment as the first Christians.

What does discipleship mean?

Being a disciple of Jesus is a tough challenge. At one stage Jesus even went so far as to say to his disciples: 'If anyone comes to me and does not hate his father and mother, his wife and children, his brothers and sisters – yes, even his own life – he cannot be my disciple.' What exactly can he have meant?

Loving Jesus first
In the time of Jesus, the Jews had a striking way of expressing the degree of love they felt for different people. Instead of saying, 'I love you more than I love him,' they would say, 'I love you and I hate him.' This was a particularly Jewish way of expressing preference in relationships, and did not literally mean that the second person was hated.

So when Jesus said these words about hating our family, he did not mean it literally! He was saying that our love for him should come so high on our list of priorities that our love even for those who are close to us will seem like hatred in comparison.

This does not mean that we give up our friendships and start to hate our families. It simply means that if there is ever a clash of loyalties, our commitment to following Jesus will always come first.

Obedience
So what does this mean in practice? At the Last Supper, which Jesus shared with his disciples the night before he died, he told them,

If you love me, you will obey what I command. John 14: 15

Love always proves itself in action. If we say that we love someone, but never show that love by pleasing them, then our love for them is not love at all. If we truly love Jesus, we will want to do what pleases him.

Today the word obedience has rather negative overtones. It can be easy to think of Jesus as some kind of dictator who wants to take away our freedom and *make* us obey him. Jesus is not like that at all, and he certainly did not treat the first disciples in that way. He wants us to stand on

This ploughman has to fix his eye on a point ahead of him, if he wants to keep his furrow straight. And a disciple of Jesus must aim steadily towards a goal – of living the life to which Jesus called him.

our own feet and learn for ourselves what it means to follow him.

It's too difficult
Discipleship for the first Christians was not easy at all, and the same is true today. If we

66 **No one who puts his hand to the plough and looks back is fit for . . . the kingdom of God.** 99

really choose to follow Jesus there may be all kinds of difficult changes we will have to make in the way we live. Some people say that discipleship is too difficult, and so they give up following Jesus. This happened with some

of Jesus' first followers, too. After Jesus had once given some difficult teaching, we read:

From this time many of his disciples turned back and no longer followed him. John 6: 66

But in a way, discipleship *should* make demands of us. Sometimes we are tempted to think that we are doing God a big favour by coming to him. We think that we can come on our own terms, ask him to clear up the mess in our lives – and then refuse to allow him to work in us as he wants. What we have to realize right from the start is that God is God, and he is in charge.

Counting the cost
Jesus never hid the fact that following him would be difficult. Instead, he told would-be followers plainly that they would have to make changes in order to follow him.

He told a rich man that he would have to give his wealth to the poor. When another man boasted about his wanting to follow Jesus, Jesus told him about the realities of living on the road, without home or security. A typical conversation of this kind went like this:

Jesus said to another man, 'Follow me.' But the man replied, 'Lord, first let me go and bury my father.' Jesus said to him, 'Let the dead bury their own dead, but you go and proclaim the kingdom of God.' Luke 9: 59, 60

Some of his replies to those who wanted to follow him sounded like cold water poured on their enthusiasm, but Jesus was concerned above all to make people see that following him meant living life a new way. And like anyone planning a new venture, they needed to count the cost before they started.

Carrying the cross
During the course of his ministry, there were many times when Jesus startled and shocked the crowd who were listening to him. But of all the things Jesus said, there can be few more shocking than these words he spoke to his disciples:

If anyone would come after me, he must deny himself and take up his cross daily and follow me. Luke 9: 23

The disciples had long thought that Jesus was leading them to immediate success and triumph, as followers of Israel's new ruler. But instead he now talked bleakly about 'carrying the cross'. Someone who carried a cross was not to be envied. He would be a convicted criminal on the way to his execution. So what did Jesus mean by saying this?

If we are to follow Jesus at all, it will mean following him by carrying the cross. Jesus was prepared to give up his own rights and privileges, even his own life, so that others should receive eternal life. So when Jesus talked about carrying the cross, he meant that we too should give up a way of life that concentrates on our own needs. Instead, we are to live as he did: serving God and putting the needs of other people before our own.

Of course, for some of Jesus' disciples, then as now, carrying the cross could mean quite literally facing death for loyalty to Jesus. There is no doubt that Jesus had this possibility in mind when he spoke these words.

In training

The demands of discipleship can seem overwhelming. But we need to remember that we will never be perfect disciples, and certainly not from the word go.

The word 'disciple' means 'one who learns' – and learning is a steady process rather than the work of a moment. To be a disciple is to become apprenticed to Jesus Christ. An apprentice learns his skills by actually practising them; not by merely reading about them.

This is exactly how Jesus worked with his first disciples. After training them for some time, he sent them out with the power to heal, cast out demons and preach the good news.

Jesus compared the kingdom of God to yeast in dough. Just a little yeast makes an amazing difference to the dough with which it is mixed. In the same way the presence of Jesus' disciples in society has an impact far beyond their apparent significance.

Another time he gave this work to seventy of his followers, sending them ahead of him in pairs. They were certainly not ready to do this, as many of them

66 **He appointed twelve . . . to be with him and to be sent out to preach.** 99

still had little understanding of who Jesus was. But this on-the-job training was enormously valuable for them. Jesus can use us too, even when we feel we are not yet capable.

A disciple is one who learns from a teacher. Christian disciples today often meet informally to learn together from the Bible.

The reward of discipleship
When the disciples came back to Jesus from this period of mission, they enthusiastically told him all that had happened. They were clearly thrilled that Jesus had trusted them enough to go out and do his work.

Luke's Gospel also tells us how Jesus reacted on his disciples' return:

At that time Jesus, full of joy through the Holy Spirit, said, 'I praise you, Father, Lord of heaven and earth, because you have hidden these things from the wise and learned, and revealed them to little children. Yes, Father, for this was your good pleasure.' Luke 10: 21

What effect does discipleship have?

Many people think that to be a Christian means to become vaguely religious. We start to go to church and do 'religious' things like praying and reading the Bible. Although Christians do all these things, they know that being a disciple goes far beyond that. To be a follower of Jesus does not mean hiding inside the church away from the difficulties of life. Quite the opposite. Being a disciple means following Jesus in the way we live the whole of our lives.

Jesus used different images to describe the impact the disciples would have on society as they progressed in their discipleship.

The light of the world
Once Jesus told his followers,

'You are the light of the world. A city on a hill cannot be hidden. Neither do people light a lamp and put it under a bowl. Instead they put it on its stand, and it gives light to everyone in the house. In the same way, let your light shine before men, that they may see your good deeds and praise your Father in heaven.'
Matthew 5: 14 – 16

This illustration certainly does not mean that we should go around boasting of our behaviour. Rather, as we follow Jesus in the way we live, we will naturally stand out in contrast to the society around us. The way we live will help others to see the way to God.

The salt of the earth
Jesus also said,

You are the salt of the earth. But if the salt loses its saltiness, how can it be made salty again? It is no longer good for anything, except to be thrown out and trampled by men.
Matthew 5: 13

Salt was extremely important in the Mediterranean world. The Romans had a proverb about salt: 'There is nothing more useful than sun and salt.' Salt was especially useful as a preservative: a vital commodity in hot countries such as Israel. It was used to keep meat from going rotten, as it was in our culture before the days of refrigeration.

So when Jesus described his disciples as 'the salt of the earth', he was saying that Christians naturally act as a preservative of all that is good in a society. A Christian is to be the kind of

> 66 Whoever tries to gain his own life will lose it; but whoever loses his life for my sake will gain it. 99

person who makes it difficult for those around him to be evil, and easy to be good.

But salt has another valuable quality: it brings out the flavour of food. Like salt, Christians should make a positive difference to the quality of life for those around them. Although we do not have all the answers to the difficulties of life, we should be able to bring hope and peace to the confused and despairing, and show the attractiveness of God in our character – through compassion, through laughter and through the enjoyment of all that God has given us. We should also be a challenge to those who are deliberately involved in evil.

Jesus' words about salt also contain a warning. If salt loses its unique qualities, then it is completely useless and will be thrown out. Jesus was saying that those disciples who did not do the work God had prepared for them in the world would similarly be useless to him.

Discipleship in the church
Discipleship is not something that I merely do on my own, 'in my small corner'. We all need the encouragement of others who are learning to be disciples themselves. We can learn a great deal from the successes and failures of other disciples.

Perhaps even more important is our need to be helped by those who are further along the road than ourselves. In the early church, older Christians undoubtedly helped younger Christians to grow into maturity in Christ. For example, the apostle Paul spoke of his relationship to a younger Christian, Timothy, as that of a father to a son. Today we need more mature Christians to

> 66 Take the teachings . . . and entrust them to reliable people, who will be able to teach others also. 99

encourage others to grow as disciples.

Jesus did not only give his teaching to the disciples. He shared his whole life with them so that they could see his teaching in action. So it is vital that more mature Christians share their lives, and not just their words. Of course there is always the danger of following the older Christian rather than Jesus himself, but it may well be that unless we follow this pattern of discipling there will not be a living church in the future.

Four steps in discipling

For those who are trying to help younger Christians grow today, these four basic steps may be useful. Obviously they are not a formula for instant success, but they can provide a structure in which more mature Christians are able to share themselves.

First, I do it, and you watch at a distance. I do not expect you to learn from me what I am not prepared to put into practice myself. What I am teaching you is not secondhand, and it is not just a theory I have learnt.

Second, I do it, and you are with me, watching, listening and possibly helping. In this way, you are able to learn without having to bear full responsibility for all that is happening.

Third, you do it, and I am right beside you to encourage you and give all the support that you need.

Fourth, you do it, and this time I am standing further back. But you can come and report back to me if necessary for further advice, help and encouragement.

This is a way in which a younger Christian can watch and learn from an older Christian's experience. Gradually the older

Christian involves the younger one until he is doing the work himself. The work might be leading a Bible study, praying with a sick person, counselling someone in difficulty or helping another person to become a Christian. It starts by being my experience of God and ends by being the other person's experience. This can be very costly to the person who is sharing his life, but it is vital for discipleship in today's church.

Discipleship can cost everything

In some cases, discipleship can cost everything. Many of the original disciples of Jesus died for their obedience to him. James the brother of John was executed in the early days of the church by Herod Agrippa. And early church tradition tells us that both Peter and Paul were put to death in Rome. The church has always been familiar with opposition and persecution.

Taking up the cross and following Jesus Christ is never easy. Not only does it bring us into collision with what we would like to do, but also it can conflict with what others expect of us. We need to remember that our discipleship can be very uncomfortable for the society in which we live.

Discipleship is a journey

Following Jesus means that we are on a journey. At the beginning of this journey we will be far from being perfect followers of Jesus Christ. Jesus does not

THE COST OF FOLLOWING JESUS

Margaret Dehqani-Tafti is the wife of the Anglican Bishop of Tehran. Together they had worked for thirty years in Iran before the revolution broke out in February 1979. Early in 1980 an attempt was made on the life of the Bishop, but he escaped. But in May of the same year their son Bahram was murdered on the outskirts of Tehran. Mrs Dehqani-Tafti said this about the experience of costly discipleship:

We had prayed for our children for twenty-four years, and I had, in my mind, in my heart, in my prayers, given my children to God to use as he felt best. And we had prayed that God would use our family for his service in Iran. But of course how could I imagine that it might cost me the life of my son? When I came to it and I had felt the pain and the suffering and the human side of it, which any parent will feel, I then realized — well, if God needed him who was I to keep him? God's generosity to me became far greater. Everything I have is from God. It made it much clearer in my mind that really our children are God's too, and we must use them and love them as God's. So the cost was great, but God's love for me is greater than that.

I think we have got to be quite clear that following Jesus is not necessarily going to be easy, not necessarily safe. And unless we are ready at the time of difficulty to continue following him, then whatever we say at other times means nothing. So often we say we love God, we want to serve God, we want to give our all, and yet we do not really do it. We hang on to ourselves, we hang on to our belongings, we hang on to the things that we have because we feel we cannot let them go.

Discipleship is deciding to follow Christ and his way. It is very easy to say things and not be sincere about them, but to be really sincere will show when troubles come. When the storm comes is the time that you have really to mean business.

expect us to arrive at our destination as soon as we start. Like a journey, following Jesus is something that takes time. We make mistakes, we take wrong turnings, but if we are determined to follow him, we will grow and become mature.

As Jesus was patient with the unsteady discipleship of his first followers, so he is patient with us today. He asks that we should be willing to follow him wherever he leads us.

4
MIRACLES

Why is there pain and suffering?

For those who work in hospitals, suffering is a part of everyday life. And although we are all familiar with pain in one way or another, when it strikes near us, we never cease to be shocked by it. We still see it as an abnormality. We begin to ask questions. Why do people suffer through sickness or accidents? Why do some people get better, while others die? And why does God not do something about it?

God's original plan

To answer those questions, we have to understand first how and why God made the world. The Bible tells us that God originally made the earth as a good place: the home in which men and women would live peacefully. God made people to live in a close and special relationship with himself – to enjoy God's company and to be free to turn to him for help. The Old Testament has many things to say about the way God planned life to work on earth.

Many passages talk about mankind as the manager of the earth. Psalm 8, in which the writer is talking to God, says,

You appointed him (mankind) ruler over everything you made; you placed him over all creation.
Psalm 8: 6

Men and women were to be responsible in using the earth's resources. God also intended people to be a support to each other. Marriage and friendship were different forms of companionship to enjoy and draw strength from. The writer of Ecclesiastes puts it like this:

Two are better off than one, because together they can work more effectively. If one of them falls down, the other can help him up.   Ecclesiastes 4: 9, 10

Rebellion against God

However, God's plan for the way people should live on the earth was ruined when people chose to follow their own way of living rather than God's. Men and women deliberately turned away from God and started to live lives that suited their own desires and ambitions. This rebellion had a number of consequences.

Estranged from God

The major consequence of rebellion against God was that we lost touch with the one who made us. A majority of people in the Western world today have little awareness of God's existence and no desire to follow the way of life he designed for us.

Many people might say that this is a good thing, that we need to be independent and to free ourselves from a restrictive belief in God. But, if the Bible record is true, then God is the one who made us and who knows exactly how we need to live. When people are out of touch with God, they often find that, underneath all the activity and achievement of their lives, everything seems to lack direction and meaning.

Spoiled relationships

Another consequence of rebellion against God can be clearly seen in today's world. People mistrust each other. Instead of two people strengthening each other through friendship, as God planned, suspicion and disagreement play a part in relationships.

The role of suspicion in human affairs can be detected at many different levels. On the personal level, misunderstanding and a lack of loyalty have contributed to the growing divorce rate in all Western countries. In society, different groups distrust each other, leading to racism and class hatred. And internationally, tensions and wars between countries are caused by a basic hostility, deeply ingrained in the human character, towards those who belong to another section of mankind.

An exploited planet

A further result of human rebellion is that we have lost touch with the world of nature. God originally appointed men and women as the managers of the earth, but we have largely failed in this responsibility. Our misunderstanding of the way nature works has led to the foolishness of building great cities like San Francisco across geological faults.

We not only misunderstand nature, we also abuse it. A large proportion of human suffering has come about through human greed which has overlooked the dangers of misusing natural resources. Chemicals handled carelessly have led to disasters like the one in Soveso in Italy, in which many people were permanently injured. And the pollution of the land, sea and air has come about through the need to dispose cheaply of industrial waste.

Why doesn't God do something?

We can see, then, that there are many ways in which our rebellion against God has brought suffering. And yet there is still an enormous area of suffering that seems to be solely God's responsibility. Why do the harvests fail and cause starvation? Why do earthquakes and floods kill people and destroy communities? Why do people die lingering deaths in hospital? Where is God in all this?

There are no simple answers to these painful questions. Anyone who has been emotionally involved in suffering – by seeing a friend or relative die, or by being in an accident of some sort – will know that trite words about 'everything working out all right in the end' do more harm than good. We all ask the question 'why?'

In search of an answer
Although there is no simple answer to the problem of pain and suffering, there are at least two pointers that may help us to make sense of the problem. First, we can never fully understand God. God is greater than our minds, and so his plans for us are bigger than we can understand. If we come to God humbly, acknowledging this fact, we may begin to understand why he allows suffering. But if we come to him in anger or pride, the chances are we will never understand.

Second, God *has* started to do something. Jesus came to reunite people with God and to show them the way they should live. He came to reverse the effects that human rebellion caused. So, too, the miracles of Jesus were God's direct response to the problem of evil and suffering in our world. He began a process that is still going on.

Why did Jesus work miracles?

In the Mediterranean world around the time of Jesus, there were many people who did, or claimed to do, miracles. They were known as 'wonder-workers', and used miracles as an impressive display of their powers. Jesus' approach to his miracles was quite different. He seemed almost reluctant to talk about them. Why then did he work miracles?

God's rule proclaimed
Jesus had come to introduce the kingdom of God, and his work advanced on many fronts. He taught a great deal about God's kingdom, using parables that showed how God's rule was working out.

Once he told a parable about a mustard seed:

The kingdom of heaven is like this. A man takes a mustard seed and sows it in his field. It is the smallest of all seeds, but when it grows up, it is the biggest of all plants. It becomes a tree, so that birds come and make their nests in its branches.
Matthew 13: 31, 32

The mustard seed was proverbial in Israel as the smallest of seeds yet it was capable of growing into the largest of all the herbs, a bush of anything up to 12 feet/3.6 metres in height. Jesus was saying that the kingdom of God begins its work in what seems like a small and insignificant way, but its potential for growth is enormous.

God's rule in action

Jesus had not come just to talk about God's kingdom; he had come to introduce it. The work of Jesus was to fight against the forces of evil at work in people and in nature. So as Jesus came into contact with people, the Gospels tell us how the kingdom

Much suffering in the world is caused by broken relationships: divided families, divided races, divided classes. We need miracles of reconciliation as well as of physical healing.

of God began its work in all sorts of 'small' ways.

Jesus told one woman that her sins were forgiven, bringing her healing and freedom from guilt. He became the friend of a chief tax-collector, Zacchaeus, who renounced his dishonest practises and repaid those he had wronged. In these, and many other ways, the rule of God was at work in people's lives and relationships.

But the kingdom of God could also be seen in the more

dramatic actions of Jesus, the miracles. The different types of Jesus' miraculous work show how he was driving back the rule of Satan in the world.

Healing diseases

Illness and disease came about through mankind's rebellion against God. Jesus lived centuries before the age of modern medicine, and every-where he travelled he met human misery in all its forms. It would have been surprising if he had not performed miracles in the face of such need. His response in healing those who were sick shows us God's concern for all those who suffer. It also shows that in his kingdom there is power to overcome suffering.

Nature miracles

There were times when Jesus calmed storms at sea, or fed large crowds of hungry people. These remarkable powers amazed those who saw them. When he had calmed a storm that threatened the safety of the disciples in their boat, we hear the disciples whispering to each other:

Who is this man? Even the wind and the waves obey him!
Mark 4: 41

Yet Jesus himself did not speak a great deal about these demonstrations of his power and authority over nature, and he discouraged his followers from attaching too much importance to them. His concern in working such miracles was to meet the needs of the moment: to overcome the fear his disciples were experiencing, or to feed hungry people.

Bringing the dead to life

In the story of Lazarus in John 11, Jesus wept as he stood outside his friend's grave. In the description of what took place, John tells us this:

Jesus was deeply moved in spirit and troubled. John 11: 33

In the language in which this was originally written, these words are unusually intense. They could just as easily be trans-lated: 'Jesus was *enraged* in spirit and troubled.' In other words, Jesus was really angry at death. He was angry at the

66 'The right time has come,' Jesus said, 'and the kingdom of God is near!' **99**

horror of death which causes so much fear and distress through-out our lives. He was angry at the way death destroys relationships and the promise of life. He was angry that death happens at all.

And most of all, he was enraged at the person who held and used the power of death – the devil himself. So Jesus ap-

SIN AND ILLNESS

What exactly is the connection between the sins we commit and the illnesses we experience? In the time of Jesus, it was widely believed that people usually became ill because of some wrong that they or their parents had done. Luke tells how Jesus healed a paralysed man. The story helps us to understand how sin and sickness are linked.

'One day when Jesus was teaching, some Pharisees and teachers of the Law were sitting there who had come from every town in Galilee and Judea and from Jerusalem. The power of the Lord was present for Jesus to heal the sick . . .'
Luke 5:17

Jesus' first words to this man were not 'Get up and walk', but 'Your sins are forgiven'. Jesus knew that this man had two needs: he needed to be healed, but he also needed to be forgiven.

This does not mean that every time we get a cold or flu it is because we have done something wrong. Rather, the New Testament teaches that human illness only exists because there is sin in the world. We live in an imperfect world, and therefore we are all liable to become ill, no matter what kind of life we lead.

But at the same time, we need to remember that sins we commit as an individual can sometimes lead to sickness. For example, if I

nurse bitterness, anger or resentment in my heart, that can express itself in many ways that not only affect my mind, but also my body.

Jesus met all the needs of the paralysed man; he healed him inside as well as outside. The New Testament has a word for his complete healing, 'salvation'. This word does not merely mean a spiritual kind of help, it means the introduction of healthiness and vitality to the whole of life — physically, mentally, socially and spiritually. Jesus is concerned that we should be healed in every part of our being.

proached Lazarus's tomb as a champion prepared for conflict. He had come to do battle with the great enemies of mankind, death and the devil. By raising the dead, Jesus showed that God's power was able to overcome the evil at work in the world.

Casting out demons
Demon-possession is hardly mentioned in the New Testament outside the Gospel accounts, and therefore it seems that the very presence of Jesus provoked an unprecedented hostility from the devil and the forces of evil. Many modern writers have suggested that people in the first century always associated illness and insanity with demon-possession, and that we can now discard this belief as a superstition. But the Gospel writers did not see demons behind every illness. They usually list demon-possession as an affliction quite separate from sickness or mental disease.

So what is demon-possession? The Gospel writers say that those whose personalities had been taken over by evil forces were demon-possessed. They were liable to periods when they had no control over their words or actions. In some isolated cases, demon-possession was said to be a cause of dumbness or epilepsy. In delivering people from this terrible condition, Jesus was attacking the very causes that bring about suffering and evil in the world, the devil and his servants.

Why Jesus did miracles
Now that we have looked at the miracles Jesus worked, we can see a number of reasons why he performed them. He worked out of compassion for those who were suffering, as a response to human need. His miracles were also the weapon he used to combat the activity of Satan, freeing people from the power of evil to live under the rule of God.

A third reason why Jesus worked miracles is shown in John's Gospel. John tells us that, through his miracles, Jesus revealed his glory as the Son of God. The miracles acted as signposts, pointing to who Jesus was.

Do the miracles prove who Jesus was?

Then some of the Pharisees and teachers of the law said to him, 'Teacher, we want to see a miraculous sign from you.' He answered, 'A wicked and adulterous generation asks for a miraculous sign!'

Many people wanted Jesus to prove who he was with a spectacular miracle that would settle things once and for all. But the response of Jesus was sharp and to the point. He consistently refused to 'perform' miracles for the sake of the authorities. He knew that miracles did not actually prove a great deal. So what was the value of the miracles for those who watched?

The raising of Lazarus
When Jesus heard that Lazarus was ill, he was far away from where his friend lived. Yet he did not go immediately to heal him, but waited instead until he had heard that Lazarus had died. The disciples were puzzled by Jesus' behaviour, but he said something which throws some light on his actions. He told them,

Lazarus is dead, and for your sake I am glad I was not there, so that you may believe. John 11: 14, 15

In other words, he wanted the disciples to see him raising

someone from death, so that their faith in him would be strengthened. This is what all miracles should do. They act as a sign pointing us to Jesus, and they encourage belief in him as God's Son.

Reactions to the miracle
Among the people who saw Jesus raising Lazarus, John tells us that there were two types of reaction to what took place. One group of onlookers put their faith in Jesus. This group seems to have been made up of people who were friends of Mary, and who therefore probably knew something of Jesus already.

But another group of people had come as some kind of observation team from Jerusalem. They reported back to the chief priests and Pharisees. John tells us that from that day on they plotted to kill Jesus.

Miracles can work in two ways
Those two opposite reactions show us that miracles on their own do not act as proof. They can encourage either greater belief or greater unbelief. For those who are already sympathetic to Jesus, who have started to believe in him, miracles can act as a powerful means of encouragement to faith. But they do not force people to believe in him; they are not proof. Those who are already against Jesus, and who see a miracle, will simply become more convinced that there is another explanation

When Jesus calmed a storm on the Sea of Galilee, it was no wonder people asked who this could be. A person with such powers must stand in a unique relationship to the created order.

of what they have seen. So miracles can also encourage greater scepticism.

The miracles as Jesus' credentials
Jesus used his miracles not as proof, but to be his credentials as the Messiah. In other words, the miracles were exactly the kind of thing people would expect the Messiah to do when he came. Jesus once used his miracles as credentials when John the Baptist was having doubts about Jesus' identity.

John, who had been imprisoned by Herod, sent two of his disciples to ask Jesus if he really was the one John had been expecting. Luke then records the following:

At that very time Jesus cured many people of their sicknesses, diseases and evil spirits, and gave sight to many blind people. He answered John's messengers, 'Go back and tell John what you have seen and heard: the blind can see, the lame can walk, those who suffer from dreaded skin-diseases are made clean, the deaf can hear, the dead are raised to life, and the Good News is preached to the poor. How happy are those who have no doubts about me!' Luke 7: 21 – 23

Jesus knew that John was discouraged in prison, that he was starting to doubt whether Jesus really was the Messiah. So, as part of his response to John's

66 Jesus called in a loud voice, 'Lazarus, come out!' 99

question, he simply continued the work he had been doing – healing, casting out demons and preaching to the poor. These activities would convince John that Jesus was doing the work of the kingdom of God.

This is how we should see the miracles today: not as proof, but as the sign that God's kingdom is at work. In that way they stimulate our faith in an active God.

Miracles today?

Many people in modern society do not believe in miracles, because they no longer believe in a God, or a spiritual dimension. And even among Christians, there are those who deny that today's church is given the power to work miracles. They believe that the gift of healing, which was given to the first apostles, was only intended for the time the apostles were alive. So do miracles still occur today?

Do miracles still happen?
Many people in the church today believe that God still gives his church the power to work miracles, and in particular the ability to heal the sick. In the last few decades there has been a renewed emphasis on the gift of healing in many different parts of the church.

Those who are involved in the ministry of healing say that the kingdom of God is still active in the world, as it was in the days of Jesus and the apostles. We can still see the activity of God's kingdom in preaching, as people come to know God's forgiveness, repent of their sins and see broken relationships healed. The New Testament gives us no reason to believe that all

these evidences of the kingdom of God should have continued, while healing should have ceased.

Why are some people not healed?
A more painful question to face is why some people are healed, while others are not. Many people have problems believing

HEALING TODAY

Reg East was one of a group of Christians who formed the Barnabas Fellowship in 1971. Reg is concerned for those in need of healing, not only physically, but also in their relationships, memories and other emotional problems. Reg East was asked some questions about healing:

In what areas of life do people most need healing today?
People need healing in their emotional and spiritual lives. We are living in a time when the whole of our social life has gone through a revolution, and this has deeply affected people. We have had two wars, which have done so much to spoil family life. And many people have lost religion as an active thing in their lives. So we find that people are now in a position where they have lost confidence in themselves and have a real sense of inadequacy. Not only are our hospitals overflowing with those who have physical illness, but our psychiatric hospitals

are full to overflowing too. So I would say that it is in the emotional and spiritual fields that the greatest need for healing is today.

Do you think the gift of supernatural healing is available to the church?
Oh, very much so. In the church's ministry of healing, we are allowing Christ to continue his healing. When he was in the world, he brought the kingdom of God, through preaching and teaching — and healing was also an integral part of his ministry. Where the kingdom of God came in, so the healing came in for spirit, mind and body. As Christians we believe that Christ is risen, alive and ascended in the glory of heaven, and that he is continuing his work through those of us who are his body. We believe and love him, and allow him to work through us.

Is it possible for the church and the medical profession to work together?
I do not think they always do, but I would think that

this would be the ideal thing. If I cut my finger, it will heal in time if I keep it clean, because the body has its own natural powers of healing that are implanted by God. They are part of our creation. The medical profession do not heal — they assist in the healing that is natural to the body. We do not heal in the church — God is the one who heals. So whether it is the medical profession or whether it is the church, we are both doing the same thing.

that Jesus actually did perform miracles, but many more have problems when God does not work a miracle for them.

It often seems that good and valuable members of the

66 **He endured the suffering that should have been ours, the pain that we should have borne.** 99

community die, while others who might not seem so deserving live on. The injustice of such suffering is extremely difficult to understand. As in all questions of human suffering, it is easier to state the problem than to suggest a solution. But the New Testament does give us some guidelines for thinking through the reasons why people are not healed.

The present and the future
One writer, Hans Küng, marvellously summed up the work of God in the world when he wrote, 'The kingdom of God is creation healed.' Jesus taught that the kingdom of God was already here, and so we see something of its healing power now. People are reconciled to each other; we start to experience something of God's new life; the sick are healed.

But Jesus also spoke about the

WHEN GOD DOES NOT HEAL

Godfrey Williams lectures in sociology at Aston University in Birmingham, England. He was diagnosed as having Hodgkins' Disease and was told possibly he had only a few months to live. Despite the prayers of many people, Godfrey was not healed. He has since died. He was asked whether he felt that this was due to any lack of faith:

Faith is not just pulling yourself up by your bootlaces and having the right sort of psychological attitude. It is a quiet confidence in God, a trust in God that he is loving, and whatever happens, that love is going to be expressed.

Faith is not like a push-button system, where if you have the right attitude you get the right answer. All prayer is a request made to a sovereign God, and he might not choose to answer our prayers in the way we would prefer him to. You are humbly asking God to change the state you are in, and you are hoping that he

will work — but he might say "no". That is an answer I think he has given me great peace to accept. And I am quite prepared to accept that in some way a greater purpose might be sustained by my death in ways I cannot understand.

kingdom not yet fully here. There is still misunderstanding and suspicion, and people remain unhealed. Because we live at a time when the kingdom of God is here, but not yet *fully* here, we will continue to see the kingdom only partially in operation. The Christian hope is in God, who has faithfully promised that one day creation will be fully healed.

God in control

The New Testament gives us a picture of God who is the master of his universe. This comes across with particular force in the book of Revelation. Surprisingly, this picture of God in Revelation was not given to Christians who had no problems and could easily see God at work. The book was addressed to Christians who were suffering violent and intense persecution at the hands of the Roman state. The New Testament sees that God is still firmly in control even when everything that is happening seems to cry out against it.

Jesus often spoke about God as a father who cares for us. When we were children we could not always understand why our parents insisted on certain things. We were taught not to

Jesus Christ's central aim was to restore things to the way they were intended in God's world. When this happens – in bodies healed or relationships mended – it brings the deepest possible happiness.

touch a hot kettle before we knew about burnt fingers. In the same way God's actions can often seem obscure, or even wrong, from our point of view.

We do not know why some people we pray for are healed while others are not. We do not know why God allows violent crimes to be committed, or why natural disasters occur. But we do know that if we could understand all that God does, he would be no bigger than our minds and not worth believing in.

The sufferings of Jesus

When we are faced with a situation that tempts us to ask why God allows us to suffer, we perhaps need to ask ourselves a deeper question. Why did God allow himself to suffer in the person of Jesus? God is not aloof and remote from our pain and difficulty. Jesus himself shows us that. Throughout his life he responded to human suffering in all its forms, giving his time and love to those who needed him.

But ultimately the greatest response of God to the sufferings of our world is seen in Jesus' death on the cross. He knew exactly what it meant to be rejected, to suffer and to die. And he was prepared to allow this to happen so that we might find the healing and wholeness that God has always intended for us.

5
LIFESTYLE

How did Jesus live?

When Jesus called his first disciples, he did not intend that they should merely sit down and listen to his teaching. He called them to do far more than that. They were to follow him by living in the same way that he lived. If we want to understand more about who Jesus was, and what it means to be a disciple of his, then we need to know how he lived.

Jesus the northerner
Jesus came from Galilee which was a thickly populated and relatively wealthy province. Galilee was proudly independent of Judea in the south, and it was the home of many of the nationalistic revolutionary movements that sprang up around the time of Jesus.

Galileans were treated with suspicion and scorn by the southerners. They were seen as uneducated, irreligious peasants who had no manners and an appalling country accent. There was a saying in Jesus' time that went: 'If anyone wishes to be rich, let him go north; if he wants to be wise, let him come south.' This prejudice against Galileans in general explains something of the Jerusalem authorities' hostility towards Jesus.

Meeting Jesus changed the lives of Galilean fishermen. In what way will he change the lifestyle of people today?

Was Jesus poor?

Although he was certainly not rich, Jesus' job as the local carpenter would have provided him with a modest but steady income. He would not have worked alone at his job, but would probably have been something like a modern-day contractor, with a number of men working under him.

The travelling preacher

Whatever financial benefits Jesus enjoyed in Nazareth, one thing is certain. He gave up the security of his job, left home and became a travelling preacher, with no guaranteed income. Life on the road was not at all easy. The parable of the good Samaritan shows that Jesus was well aware of the dangers of travel.

Jesus did not hide the difficulties of the life he led from those who wanted to follow him. Once he said to a would-be follower,

Foxes have holes and birds of the air have nests, but the Son of man has no place to lay his head. Matthew 8. 20

How did Jesus and the disciples live?

Jesus and his closest followers depended entirely for their living on the giving and hospitality of those who were sympathetic towards them, like Mary and Martha at Bethany. In Jewish society at the time, this was a perfectly legitimate way for a Rabbi and his disciples to exist.

Luke's Gospel gives us a vivid picture of Jesus on the road with his followers, and tells us how they were supported:

Jesus travelled about from one town and village to another, proclaiming the good news of the kingdom of God. The Twelve were with him, and also some women who had been cured of evil spirits and diseases: Mary (called Magdalene) from whom seven demons had come out; Joanna the wife of Cuza, the manager of Herod's household; Susanna; and many others. These women were helping to support them out of their own means. Luke 8: 1 – 3

Judas Iscariot was in charge of the money they had, which they shared between them. And although they were not well-off, it seems that some of their money was used to give to the poor. Other followers of Jesus provided him with hospitality. During the final week of his life when Jesus was in Jerusalem, he stayed in the home of Mary and Martha in nearby Bethany

What did the disciples give up?

A rich young man once came to Jesus and asked him what he needed to do to receive eternal life. Jesus told him,

Go and sell all you have and give the money to the poor, and you will have riches in heaven; then come and follow me. Mark 10: 21, 22

Does this mean, then, that all who wish to follow Jesus must make the same kind of sacrifice?

Jesus did not set rigid rules for all who wanted to follow him. But he knew what each person would have to give up in order to give his first loyalty to Jesus. Sometimes he did tell people to give away their possessions, and others were told to leave their jobs. Jesus may still expect this in specific circumstances today. But other followers of Jesus, such as Joseph of Arimathea, remained rich, while Peter and Matthew still owned houses.

Things had to be given up if they were a threat to true discipleship. Jesus' attitude to wealth and possessions was summed up when he said,

'Do not store up riches for yourselves here on earth, where moths and rust destroy, and robbers break in and steal. Instead, store up riches for yourselves in heaven, where moths and rust cannot destroy, and robbers cannot break in and steal. For your heart will always be where your riches are.'
Matthew 6: 19 – 21

Who did Jesus mix with?

Jesus was an unusual figure in Jewish society, because he refused to behave in the way people expected a Rabbi to behave. While he was quite capable of debating the finer

THE GREATEST AFFLICTION

Jean Vanier founded a community in France called L'Arche — the Ark. In this community mentally disabled people live alongside mentally able people as equals and not as social rejects. Jean Vanier believes that the mentally disabled have many gifts to share with those around them and that they are not the people most afflicted in society:

The greatest suffering is not an afflicted person. I was speaking yesterday to a lady who is blind, a Prioress of a Convent — a very beautiful person. But it always strikes me how sometimes blind people see very clearly

inside. The tragedy is not that this girl is blind — that is not serious. What is serious is a heart that is made to love and does not, and seeks to possess. All the wars and the catastrophes and sufferings of the world — they come from hardness of heart and selfishness, and so on.

The sufferings of our men here do not come from encephalitis or meningitis or the fact that their mother had German measles or that there was a mishap during their birth. It is the fact that they are rejected, that is the worst thing. The greatest affliction is to reject someone. It is even

greater than to be rejected, because in a way it shows some terrible sickness of the heart.

I think the important thing is for us all to say, well, what am I called to do today? Where am I in the situation where I am? Who are the people that I am rejecting and not looking at? And how can my heart open up a tiny bit more to welcome? It is not even to say what project can I get involved in — this is not the most important issue. How can I, today, at my home, at my little community life, my family life, become open to a rejected person?

points of the Law with the scribes in the Temple, he also did the unthinkable: he talked with prostitutes, ate with the most corrupt tax-collectors, and

> ❝ Will a person gain anything if he wins the whole world but loses his life? ❞

generally associated with those who were social outcasts.

Jesus had time for the ordinary people – those who were unknown and uncared for – and he refused to allow social conven-tion to get in the way of real human need. But he was also unafraid to be seen with the rich, and often accepted the hospitality and friendship of the Pharisees and others in authority.

The lifestyle of Jesus
Jesus attracted attention and stirred up opposition not only through his radically different teachings, but also because of a radically different way of life. He could urge his followers not to depend on possessions because he himself did not depend on them. Jesus gives us a living example of his own teaching.

What did Jesus teach about lifestyle?

From Jesus' teaching, it sometimes looks as if, to be his follower, we have to sell all that we have, give away our money, leave our homes and jobs and live in dependence on the generosity of other people. Is this what Jesus asks of *all* his disciples? Before we can answer this, we need to ask a number of other questions.

Surely things are different today
The age we live in is completely different from the age Jesus lived in. In the area of lifestyle, we face many pressures today that did not exist in first-century Palestine.

We live in what has been called 'the consumer society', where everyone is encouraged to improve the quality of their lives by *having* more. The adverts tell us that labour-saving devices will make our lives easier; cosmetics will make us more attractive; tobacco will somehow give us access to a high-flying society of the rich and beautiful. The happy, fulfilled life consists of more money, more possessions, sexual attractiveness and financial security.

Because Jesus did not have to face all these pressures, and did not live in a consumer society like ours, we are entitled to ask whether his teaching on lifestyle is still relevant. Should we even try to apply his first-century teaching to twentieth-century problems?

Some things do not change
Although the details of life in Jesus' time were very different from those in twentieth-century society, there are many basic similarities. For example, the desire for greater wealth and for ownership was as deeply rooted in society then as it is now. There may not have been advertising to capitalize on those basic desires, but human covetousness was still there.

And many of the problems faced by modern society were present in the time of Jesus. In the first century, Judea and Galilee were troubled areas. They faced high taxation, inflation, and even low productivity. In addition, Palestine was over-populated. So we should not think of the problems we face as unique to our time.

We need to be careful, of course, when reading the words of Jesus, not to take them out of the context of their time. But once we have understood exactly what Jesus was talking about, then we will be able to work out his meaning for us today.

Keeping up appearances
So what did Jesus have to say about lifestyle? At the root of Jesus' message was the concern not merely to change the way people *behave*, but to change what people *are*. Once this had happened their behaviour would naturally be different. Often when Jesus talked with people he challenged their hidden motives to show them that they needed to change inside. Once, a man in the crowd following Jesus asked him to help in sorting out a will. Immediately, Jesus replied,

Watch out! Be on your guard against all kinds of greed; a man's life does not consist in the abundance of his possessions.
Luke 12: 15

And Jesus was ruthlessly honest with other people such as the Pharisees, who loved to make a great display of their goodness. To them he said,

Woe to you, teachers of the law and Pharisees, you hypocrites! You are like whitewashed tombs, which look beautiful on the outside, but on the inside are full of dead men's bones and every-thing unclean. In the same way, you appear to people as righ-teous, but on the inside you are full of hypocrisy and wickedness.
Matthew 23: 27, 28

So what is a Christian?
If Jesus was not out merely to change the outward appearances of people, then what does it mean

to be his follower? Many of the ideas around today on what it means to be a Christian seem to centre on the notion of outside change.

Some think that a Christian is a person who believes in certain

66 **From within, out of men's hearts, come . . . all these evils.** 99

things, such as God and the church; others that Christians are people who do good to others, who help out in difficult situations. Christians are respectable, decent and upright citizens – or

Being a Christian is meant to make a difference, not just on Sunday, but from Monday to Saturday as well. Ordinary everyday life is the setting in which a distinctively Christian approach has to be worked out.

perhaps they are people who have no fun in their lives and would like to make the rest of us the same.

While it is obvious that some of these ideas are wrong, others do seem to be on the right track. Surely a Christian is someone who believes in God and puts himself out for the sake of other people?

The heart of the matter
Christians believe and do certain things, certainly, but that is not

the complete picture, or even the most important part of the picture. A Christian is not just someone who does things in a particular way or believes in particular facts. A Christian is someone who is willing to be changed by Jesus Christ.

Jesus came to call those who were in need and who were prepared to admit they were in need. The Pharisees once complained to Jesus about his habit of eating with the despised members of society. He replied,

It is not the healthy who need a doctor, but the sick. I have not come to call the righteous, but sinners to repentance.
Luke 5: 31, 32

The problem is that many people, like the Pharisees, refuse to admit that they are sick and need Christ's help. We hide behind barriers of pride and respectability and think that we can cope on our own. But Christians are people who are prepared to admit that they are not perfect, and that their motives are not always pure – and who then come to Jesus to be made fully healthy.

New attitudes
So Jesus is not interested primarily in making us respectable, nor even in changing our outward behaviour. He is concerned to change our inside life: our attitudes, motives, desires, feelings and so on. A person may change outwardly – but only because he feels he *ought* to, or to show other people how religious he is. If he does it for that reason, reading the Bible will do him little good. The impact comes when a person reads the Bible because he longs to know God more.

So until our inside nature and attitude is really changed nothing significant will have altered. That is why Jesus kept on going back to the root of the matter. He knew that outward change is useless unless it springs from an inward change.

God as Father
A new dimension we will begin to develop as Jesus works in us is seeing God as our Father: the one who provides for all our needs and is concerned about all we do. When we start to see God in this way, we are freed from the contemporary way of looking

❝ The Son of man . . . came to serve and to give his life to redeem many people. ❞

at wealth, possessions, social status and security. Because we are no longer totally dependent on these things for our happiness, they cease to have the same vital importance for us.

This does not mean that we can become irresponsible with money, but that we put it in its right place in our order of priorities. We may want to give some of our money away, and become the means by which God provides for other people. And thinking of God as our Father does not make us unconcerned if we have no job. But it does save us from despair in that situation.

This attitude is not an easy one to hold on to especially if we are poor or out of work, and when God does not seem to care for us. But Jesus challenged even the poor of his time not to become anxious about the circumstances of their life:

Therefore I tell you, do not worry about your life, what you will eat or drink; or about your body, what you will wear. Is not life more important than food, and the body more important than clothes? Look at the birds of the air; they do not sow or reap or store away in barns, and yet your heavenly Father feeds them. Are you not much more valuable than they? Matthew 6: 25, 26

Serving each other

Another new attitude that we see in the life of Jesus concerns the way that we look at other people. Modern-day living has often been described as 'the rat-race'. We have been brought up to see other

Our lifestyle should not simply reflect the pattern of the society around us. The needs and inequalities of the world point us towards a level of simplicity, not too weighed down by the clutter of modern life.

people as competitors rather than as neighbours. The way in which Jesus treated those around him was completely different. Once he took a bowl of water and a towel and washed the feet of all his disciples. Then, he said to them,

I, your Lord and Teacher, have just washed your feet. I have set an example for you, so that you will do just what I have done for you.
John 13: 14, 15

So following Jesus means not only a new way of seeing God, but also a new way of relating to people. We cannot think of our discipleship as some private affair that concerns only me and God. To be a Christian will involve us in serving each other in the same way that Jesus served the needs of those around him.

Honesty about ourselves
Jesus also spoke about a change of attitude in the way we look at ourselves. Often we feel that we have to prove ourselves in front of other people, even before God. We may have masks that

Jesus' life was one of service to others. To follow him is not some grandiose notion, but a matter of laying ourselves open to the needs of others.

encourage others to think of us as competent, self-assured and decent. Jesus spoke about God as the one who knows all our secrets and weaknesses – and yet still loves us. We cannot pretend with God, and he encourages us not to pretend with ourselves or in front of others.

Jesus accepted the friendship and loyalty of his first disciples despite the fact that they had many fears and reservations about following him. In the same way he accepts our imperfect discipleship. When we accept that Jesus accepts us, with all our faults, and longs to make us more like himself, then we will be ready to be changed by him.

God's patience
These three basic changes in attitude (in the way that we look at God, other people, and ourselves) will not come about overnight. The attitudes we have now took years to form, and to change them is the work of a lifetime. God knows this, and is patient in helping us to see our weaknesses and overcome them. But we can never hope to love in the way Jesus did until God has begun these basic changes of attitude inside us.

How should we live?

Jesus turned the accepted norms of society upside down. He said that life in the kingdom of God was a reversal of the standards and priorities most people take for granted. Accepting this can be a painful process as it often cuts right across the way that we like to behave, and the way that other people like us to behave. So what does following the lifestyle of Jesus mean in practical terms?

Simplicity
Because of our dependence on God, we are able to live more simply, free from worry and the pressures that many face in the rat-race. In practice, though, many Christians feel the same pressures and worries as everyone else. We need deliberately to make our lives more simple so that they accurately reflect our trust in God's generosity.

This might well mean eating more simply, making do without spending so much on clothes, sharing our resources (such as a car, or other equipment), and learning to borrow and lend instead of to buy and sell. In these and other ways, our money and resources will become avail-

CHRISTIAN ACTION FOR THE POOR

Ron Sider is the author of the book Rich Christians in an Age of Hunger, *about Christians responsibility towards the poor and the oppressed. He was asked:*

To what extent is God on the side of the poor and oppressed in the world?
I think God is on the side of the poor and the oppressed, and I think that is one of the central teachings of the Bible. However, I think that we have to be careful at that point. When I say that God is on the side of the poor, I do not mean that it is a good thing to be poor. It is not. I do not mean that the poor are automatically in a right relationship with God. Poor people need to come into a living relationship with Jesus Christ just like middle-class sinners. But the Bible teaches very clearly that God has a very special concern for the poor. There are very many scriptures which say that God is at work in history casting down the rich when they simply neglect the poor.

Does the church in Western society share Jesus' attitude to the poor?
I think one of the greatest tragedies in the church today is that Jesus' attitude towards the poor is not the dominant, common one in the church. I do not feel good about saying it, but it seems to me that most people in churches in the West are largely unconcerned about the poor. They are concerned about a higher standard of living next year, they are concerned about larger houses, better cars, more gadgets, but they are not very concerned about the poor. I think if we are going to follow Jesus in our time, then we need to go back to Jesus' special concern for the poor and really follow him at that point.

What can individual Christians do to help the poor?
There are lots of ways in which we can reduce our personal lifestyle. I am not talking about poverty. I do not live in poverty, and I do not think poverty is the call for the average person who believes in Christ. But we can spend less on clothes, we can spend less on housing, we can spend less on transportation — and in many different ways we can spend less on ourselves and increase the amount we have to share with others. Of course, if we simply put that money in the bank, then it does not help at all. But if we give the money that we save to organizations working to reduce poverty in the Third World, then of course that money can be directly helpful.

How should local churches reduce their lifestyle?
I think in a number of ways. In our local congregation we can have a 'special things' cupboard, where things that are used only occasionally (certain kinds of garden tools or other equipment) can be placed, and anyone who needs to use them for a given week can arrange to do so. A local congregation can also decide that they as a body will study both what the Bible says about the poor and about the needs of the world. That can be a common important theme for that congregation for two years. I think that local congregations can also decide that they are going to spend as much money outside the church as they do in the church. I wish that every congregation would decide that when there needs to be church construction of some sort they would always have a matching fund that would equal what they are spending on their church buildings. That equal matching fund would then be sent abroad for evangelism and justice.

able for more important things, such as giving to those who really need help.

Christians are not just 'nice'
Christians are not called by Jesus to become nice people, but new people, who stand out in a society because they are different. He once gave three examples of the difference in behaviour he means:

If someone strikes you on the right cheek, turn to him the other also. And if someone want to sue

Jesus came from Nazareth, in the northern province of Galilee. He lacked the sophistication of one brought up in Jerusalem.

you and take your tunic, let him have your cloak as well. If someone forces you to go one mile, go with him two miles.
Matthew 5: 39 – 41

All these responses are much more than merely being nice to people who act unpleasantly. Jesus was not saying 'Be nice'. He was calling people to a radically different method of living. Being slapped on the right cheek was the backhanded slap, a calculated insult punishable at law. To take someone's jacket was expressly forbidden in the Old Testament. And to go an extra distance for a Roman soldier was not compulsory; to do so would be actively to help the enemy occupying forces.

By giving these three examples Jesus was showing that the attitudes and values of

❝ Happy are you poor; the kingdom of God is yours! ❞

God's kingdom are totally diffe-rent from those of the world. Those who conform to the kingdom of God will find them-selves nonconformists in society.

Christians and the poor
Jesus spent a great deal of time in the company of those who were poor, powerless and

rejected. And in many ways he broke the social rules of his time to do this. He obviously saw helping the poor as a vital part of his mission.

There were many in Jewish society, as there are today, who were themselves rich, and who callously neglected the poor. Jesus had angry words for this sort of attutude. There is a parable he told which begins with these words:

There was once a rich man who dressed in the most expensive clothes and lived in great luxury every day. There was also a poor man named Lazarus, covered with sores, who used to be brought to the rich man's door, hoping to eat the bits of food that fell from the rich man's table. Even the dogs would come and lick his sores. Luke 16: 19 – 21

The anger with which Jesus spoke these words is directed at us if we have that same cold approach towards those who are poor today.

As Christians we should not only give money to the needs of the poor, although that is impor-tant. We need to give our time, as Jesus did, in helping those neglected by society. And we should also work to fight the injustices that create unloved people, or people who do not have enough to eat.

Loving my neighbour
According to the parable of the Good Samaritan in Luke 10, my

neighbour may well be someone I do not find it easy to get on with, or I may be prejudiced against him for one reason or another. If that is the case, then I have to learn to go out of my way to care for that person. Christian love means to be willing to understand other people, to spend time with them, to listen to their

In the Western world, we greatly value privacy and an individual approach to life. But Jesus called people into a community, who would live a shared life and rate each other's interests as highly as their own.

needs and care for them in practical ways.

Just as we do not choose the neighbours in the street where

we live, so we cannot choose whom we will and will not serve. Rather we choose to be a servant, and allow God to show us whom we are to serve. Practically, this means giving hospitality to those who cannot return it, loving those who hate us, speaking to those who hold a grudge against us.

To do all this goes against the grain for most people. We feel we have a right to nurse grievances, to take our revenge, to keep hold

❝ Love your neighbour as you love yourself. ❞

of our prejudices. To become a good neighbour in the sense that Jesus talked about will therefore be hard work. When we find it impossibly hard, then we should be willing to come to Jesus,

confess our weakness and prejudice, and ask him to change our attitude towards that person.

New priorities
To belong to the kingdom of God is to put human nature into reverse. Where once my primary concern was for myself, my bank account, my reputation, my promotion prospects or my possessions, now my concerns will be directed increasingly outside myself.

In talking about the claims that money and possessions make on our attention, Jesus spoke about the greatest priority for his followers. He said,

Instead (of worrying about food and clothes), be concerned above everything else with the kingdom of God and with what he requires of you, and he will provide you with all these other things.
Matthew 6: 33

6
PRAYER

What is prayer?

In the life of Jesus and the first disciples, prayer played a vitally important part. To them, prayer was not merely another activity; it was crucial to their involvement in all that God was doing. Because of this emphasis on prayer in the New Testament, it is important to ask exactly what prayer is, and to discover for ourselves its importance.

A psychological trick?
Some people see prayer as something done by people who cannot cope with the pressures of modern life. They argue that as there is no God, those who pray are simply reassuring themselves that there is meaning to the things that happen to them. Prayer helps to cushion them from the dreadful realities of life.

And yet prayer is often not a comforting experience at all. For many Christians, prayer is a constant struggle; it is not always pleasant, and makes demands on the one who prays. Christians believe that prayer is much deeper than psychological manipulation. They believe in a God who often upsets cherished plans through prayer.

Archbishop William Temple was once criticized by people who said that answers to prayer were no more than coincidence. He replied, 'When I pray, coincidences happen: when I don't, they don't.' Christians still believe that prayer changes people and events, and not only the one who prays. Prayer is

therefore a key element in the Christian faith.

Children and prayer
Most of us prayed as children. We were used to having complete faith in our parents, and so could have that same kind of trust in God. The quality of trust that a child has is at the root of all prayer. Once, the disciples tried to stop parents bringing their children to Jesus. He responded by saying,

Let the children come to me, and do not stop them, because the kingdom of God belongs to such as these. I assure you that whoever does not receive the kingdom of God like a child will never enter it. Mark 10: 14, 15

The New Testament tells us that we should grow up in our understanding of God, but we should never lose the quality of trust that children have. This does not mean that prayer is a childish activity that we can leave behind, as so many do, as we grow up. It means that children have something that we lose as we grow older. We need to regain our ability to trust God completely.

Prayer is a relationship

Jesus was unusual in his time in teaching his disciples to think of God as their Father. He also taught them to call God 'Father' in their prayers, and the original word he used, 'Abba', literally means 'Daddy'. Clearly Jesus meant his followers to think of God in a particularly intimate way.

In the relationship that a Christian has with God, prayer plays the all-important role of communication. If someone were to say that he was a good friend of someone else, but that they never met or spoke to each other, we would suspect that they had no relationship at all. In the same way, prayer is as vital to our relationship with God as meeting and talking is to any human relationship.

Giving and receiving

By giving our time to God in prayer, we make ourselves available to him, and can give to him and receive from him. Through prayer we give him our praise for who he is and what he means to us. And we give him our thanks for what we know he has done for us and for other people.

We also receive through

CHILDREN AT PRAYER

Lord, I ask you
to help those
who lost
their houses,
their crops
and everything that belonged to them.
Help me also
to pass
in the school,
not only me,
but also my friends.
I thank you for everything
that you have given us.

Marcia Haberkamp, aged 11, from Brazil

I give thanks to God
because he has not left me alone in the world,
that I have a family that I love very much
and that they love me also.
I would like it if everyone in the world
had a family and that being together

could feel the warmth of love and care
the same as I feel.
Almighty God, I would like that there would be
no more hungry children in the world,
that people would stop thinking of killing
and would help the people that are so poor.
Amen

Elsie Irizarry Afandor, aged 13, from Puerto Rico

Lord, I pray for my poor father.
He works so hard and tries so hard to help
my mother and us the children.
But his salary is so small he cannot do all
the things he wants to do for us.
Help us to be good children who love him,
and who will encourage him
to keep his trust in you.
Some day, we believe,
everything will be all right.

Victoria Mulbah, aged 12, from Liberia

'Knock, and the door will be opened to you, Jesus said. In prayer we come to God with our deepest desires, believing that he will not condemn or exclude us.

prayer. We receive power for living and an understanding of what God is doing in our lives. Sometimes a tragedy may happen close to us, and one sure way of being confused and bewildered by it is not to be in touch with God by regularly praying. Through prayer, we also receive God's forgiveness as we are honest in his presence and admit our sins.

What prayer is not

Prayer is not a means of twisting God's arm. It is easy to think that, because we have spent some time praying that a certain thing will happen, God *ought* to do what we have asked. Just because a man has prayed for guidance about a girl he would like to go out with, that does not mean he can then feel God *has* guided him to do so!

Neither is prayer a way to let other people know how religious we are. Jesus told an amusing story about a pompous Pharisee who knows that all Jews are required to pray at 3 p.m. So he arranges his day so as to be in the most public place in town at that time, and then loudly and impressively praises God with outstretched arms. That is *not* what prayer is about, said Jesus. Prayer should never be used to show off our relationship with the Almighty.

The friend at midnight

On a positive note, Jesus also taught how we should be insistent in asking God for our needs. Painting the picture of another character, he told the story of the grumpy friend at midnight:

Suppose one of you should go to a friend's house at midnight and say to him, 'Friend, let me borrow three loaves of bread. A friend of mine who is on a journey has just come to my house, and I haven't got any food for him!' And suppose your friend should answer from inside, 'Don't bother me! The door is already locked, and my children and I are in bed. I can't

get up and give you anything.'
Well, what then? I tell you that
even if he will not get up and give
you the bread because you are
his friend, yet he will get up and
give you everything you need
because you are not ashamed to
go on asking.   Luke 11 : 5 - 8

God's willingness to give
Jesus told that story to tell us
about God's *willingness* to give to
us. Jesus meant that if a grumpy
friend will get up at midnight and
give you what you need, how
much more will God, who loves
to be generous, give to you when
you ask. The whole parable
focuses on the fact that the sleepy
friend eventually got up and gave
what was needed. And Jesus

*The quality of God which the Bible speaks
of most frequently is his 'grace'. God's
grace is his readiness to give freely. So
when we pray to him, we are approaching,
not a reluctant bureaucrat, but a supremely
generous father.*

pointed out that God is much
more willing to give to us than
that grumpy and sleepy
neighbour.

But the other side to the story
is that we need to ask and go on
asking God for what we need.
Jesus said that God gives to us as
we ask. And, like the friend in the
parable, we should ask
persistently and without
embarrassment. To keep on
asking for something does not
mean that we think God is deaf,
or reluctant to give. He calls us to

persist in prayer because he wants us actively to seek his help.

Confidence in God
Jesus ended the parable by saying,

Would any of you who are fathers give your son a snake when he asks for fish? Or would you give him a scorpion when he asks for an egg? Bad as you are, you know how to give good things to your children. How much more, then, will the Father in heaven give the Holy Spirit to those who ask him! Luke 11: 11 – 13

As a father gives his son what is good, so we can be confident in prayer that God looks after our best interests. To pray in this way is to have trust in a good God, who is bigger than all our needs.

What can Jesus teach us about prayer?

The disciples had been brought up to pray in the synagogue from childhood. Yet when they saw Jesus praying one day, he obviously made a deep impression on them, because they asked him, 'Teach us to pray'. There must have been something different about the way in which Jesus prayed. So what can we learn from Jesus' habits of prayer?

Early in the morning

Very early the next morning, long before daylight, Jesus got up and left the house. He went out of the town to a lonely place, where he prayed. Mark 1 : 35

The Gospel writers show us that Jesus continued this habit throughout his public life.

 Many of us find this example very difficult to follow, and obviously it is not a rigid rule. For some people it is quite impossible, because of young children, or jobs with difficult hours. But for those for whom it is a possibility, starting the day with God in this way can be a battle worth winning.

Before big decisions

At that time Jesus went up a hill to pray and spent the whole night there praying to God. When day came, he called his disciples to him and chose twelve of them . . .
Luke 6: 12, 13

We often need God's specific guidance over all sorts of practical decisions – a new job, moving from one place to another. At such times it can be valuable to put some time aside for special prayer, as Jesus did before calling his disciples.

Facing temptation

Jesus said to them, 'Keep watch, and pray that you will not fall into temptation. The spirit is willing, but the flesh is weak.'
Mark 14: 38

Jesus said this to his disciples in the Garden of Gethsemane, immediately before his arrest. But in the end he prayed, while they fell asleep – with the result that he was able to go through great suffering and death, while they were filled with fear and confusion. In the same way, we can face temptation with strength when we pray

In need of God's encouragement

After all the people had been baptized, Jesus also was

HOW IMPORTANT WAS PRAYER TO JESUS?

Some thoughts from Dr Howard Marshall:
Jesus was brought up in a pious Jewish home, and so it would have been natural for him to pray to God from his earliest days, perhaps at fixed times of the day. And in the Gospels we find that he certainly was a person who prayed frequently. There is the well-known story of him going into the Temple at the age of twelve, and staying behind there while his parents went home without him. He said that he wished to be in the house of his Father. This intimate way in which he talked about God as his Father suggests that he prayed to God and felt he had a personal relationship with him.

All the Gospels tell us that Jesus prayed, but it is Luke who lays the most emphasis on it and brings out the fact that Jesus prayed at particular occasions in his life. Luke, for example, tells us that Jesus prayed when he was being baptized by John at the River Jordan, and that he prayed on the Mount of Transfiguration. It is Luke who tells us that Jesus told Peter he was praying especially for him, so that his faith would not fail in the trial that lay ahead of him. And it is Luke who tells us that Jesus prayed for the people who were crucifying him: 'Father, forgive them, for they don't know what they are doing.'

In the Gospel of Luke, as in the other Gospels, Jesus tells his disciples that they are to pray, and they see him as an example to follow. There is a passage in Luke's Gospel where Jesus was praying by himself and his disciples came to him and said, 'Lord, we want you to teach us how to pray.' And in answer to their requests Jesus gave them what we call the Lord's Prayer, and then taught them about prayer. Luke alone has a story which tells about two men who went into the Temple to pray: one in a proud attitude, full of himself and telling God how good he was, the other man conscious of his weakness and failure and simply confessing to God how unworthy he was. Jesus said it was the second man who was heard by God, not the first. And that is the attitude in which Jesus wants us to pray also.

baptized. **While he was praying, heaven was opened, and the Holy Spirit came down upon him in bodily form like a dove.**
Luke 3: 21, 22

At three key points of his life – during his baptism, at his transfiguration, and before his arrest – Luke tells us that it was while Jesus was praying that he

❝ One of his disciples said to Jesus, 'Lord, teach us to pray'. ❞

was encouraged by God. This does not mean that prayer is *always* encouraging, but God can specially meet with us when we give him our time and attention.

Many people find it hard to pray alone. There is great encouragement in getting together to pray informally.

Concern for others

Simon, Simon! Listen! Satan has received permission to test all of you, to separate the good from the bad, as a farmer separates the wheat from the chaff. But I have prayed for you, Simon, that your faith will not fail.
Luke 22: 31, 32

Jesus expressed his concern for Simon Peter by praying for him. It is easy for us to turn our concern for others into gossip or criticism. If only we prayed as much as we criticized, then God's love would flow between us, and the devil would not be able to divide us.

There are no rules in prayer
Having looked at the example of Jesus, it is extremely important to stress that Jesus himself did not lay down any cast-iron rules

about praying, and neither should we. God understands the pressures we are under, and while he wants us to work at prayer and not give up, at the same time he does not want us to feel guilty because we fall short of our own expectations.

There has been a great stress in recent times on the need for regular routine in prayer, and as a result many people have found prayer a kind of slavery as they consistently fail to pray in the expected way and at the expected times. Formal routines of prayer are no guarantee of success, and the busy person who learns to pray while working can be as fresh spiritually as the person who rigidly prays early each morning.

Why is prayer so difficult?

The subject of prayer often makes people feel guilty because they have always found it uphill going. Although most Christians have periods when prayer is an enjoyable and uplifting experience, prayer is usually something of a struggle. So why do we find prayer so hard?

The devil's opposition
The devil's strategy is always to spoil the relationship we enjoy with God. Because prayer is such an important part of that relationship, it is bound to be a target for the devil's activity. Often he will try to stop us from praying by accusing us of some sin we have committed and telling us that we are not worthy to come before God. He tries to convince us that God no longer loves us because of our sins.

Dread at approaching God
In accusing us in this way, the devil is aggravating a feeling that we all have in approaching God. We naturally find it hard consciously to enter God's presence, because we are sinful people coming before a holy God. We know that we fail to live up to his standards, and so we feel naked and inadequate before him.

When feelings such as these prevent us from praying, we need to remember that Jesus came and died so that we could come to God for the forgiveness we need. It is only as we are honest with God, admit our inadequacy and ask for the help of the Holy Spirit in our prayers that God will forgive and strengthen us.

Superficiality
In an age where there is an emphasis on the 'instant', to pray consistently over long periods of time is not an appealing

prospect. Also, many of the things we do are evident to other people and make us appreciated. The best kind of prayer is often done quietly, behind the scenes, noticed by no one but God himself. So prayer can seem boring in the whirl of twentieth-century life.

Spiritually, our age is unfit. We need to think of prayer as an activity that needs regular exercise. As we do so, we will be able to give our best to God.

Prayer and our feelings
One of the greatest discouragements to prayer is the

66 **We do not know how we ought to pray; the Spirit himself pleads with God for us.** 99

feeling that God is distant and unconcerned, and we seem to be praying to ourselves. To continue

to pray at times like that is extremely difficult, and many people give up altogether until they can feel something of God's presence again. But it is important to remember that prayer does not rely for its effectiveness on our feelings; it is based on the fact that God is our Father, and the promise of Jesus that God hears us when we pray.

We do not know how to pray
Prayer can easily be stalled when we are confronted with a situation that we feel we should pray about, but find that we simply cannot. Paul the apostle once said that we do not know how to pray, and therefore we need to ask the Spirit of God to teach us what we should pray in difficult situations. The Holy Spirit can help us in all the difficulties of our Christian life, but especially in the whole realm of the weakness we often feel in prayer.

How can we develop in prayer?

Just as with any human activity, we need to give our time and energy in developing our approach to prayer. Often we feel defeated by our failures in prayer, and give up. So how can we positively develop a habit of prayer?

Preparing for prayer

Jesus went out of his way to go to a quiet place alone and pray. In the same way, when we consciously turn our attention towards God, itns good to allow ourselves to let go of whatever we have just been doing, to relax

66 **Be joyful always, pray at all times, be thankful in all circumstances.** 99

and become aware of the person we are approaching – God himself.

Often we rush before God with noisy minds, full of things to ask him to do. We forget that the prime purpose of prayer is to be with God, to enjoy him and to allow him to speak with us. We need to allow ourselves time to tune in to God.

Listening to God

We live in a busy age and so it is important to spend time listening to God rather than merely pouring out our requests to him straight away. He may have

something he wants us to reflect on, he may want to encourage us with his love. Listening takes time, but rushed prayer often allows us no opportunity to hear what God is saying to us.

One way of listening to God is to be quite still before him and to meditate. Many Christians fear meditation as a product of Eastern religions. But meditation has a long history in the church, and is quite different from Eastern meditation in which the mind is emptied. In Christian meditation, we focus our attention on God himself, on a verse or passage of the Bible, or on a symbol that points us to God. In this way, we allow God to speak to our deepest needs.

Variety in prayer

If we find prayer difficult or plain boring, the reason may be that we are not varied enough in our praying. If a boy met his girl friend at the same time, in the same place, and said the same words to her for the same length of time each day, their relationship would soon grow stale. Christianity at its heart is a love-relationship with Jesus

THE EXPERIENCE OF PRAYER

Metropolitan Anthony Bloom, of the Russian Orthodox church in London, England, proved the effectiveness of a life of prayer as an army surgeon in wartime before he became a church leader.

Would you say that there is a great deal more to prayer than simply asking God to do things?
There is a great deal more, but usually there is this idea that there is a hierarchy in praying — the lowest being petition, then intercession (asking for others), then thanksgiving, then praise. But I do not think it is as simple as this, because thanksgiving is a very simple thing. When you have received something, to say thankyou does not require any faith. You have the bird in hand. Praise, at moments when you are aware of the greatness and holiness of God, is simple. What is much more difficult, and in a way requires a much greater faith — a concreteness of faith — is petition and intercession, with the certainty that God can hear and God can respond. Thanksgiving comes after the event. Petition requires the certainty that you have a God of love and that he communes with you.

So if God always hears our prayers, why does he not always answer?

We may be like children, who ask something from their parents. The parents know perfectly well that if they give it, it will do more harm than good. I remember an old American who was a scoutmaster when I was a boy, who spoke to us about prayer. He said that for years he prayed for God to give him the gift of taking his teeth out every evening as his grandfather could do, and he added, 'Thanks be to God, he refused my request until the last years of my life!' Well, very often our praying amounts to that kind of thing. We ask for something that is too

transient, too small for our greatness, not only God's.

Do you think that when God says 'No' to our prayers, we are tempted to think that is not an anwer?
Yes; it happens because very primitively people who claim to be believers imagine that because they have ended their prayer by saying, 'And this we ask in Jesus Christ's name', the answer must be 'Yes'. But it is not so simple. To ask in Christ's name means to ask with the intention that my prayers should be that of Christ if he were here in my place. It is not a way of forcing God's hand. When Christ says, 'Whatever you ask in my name, it shall be done to you', it does not mean we can force his hand by saying, 'It is in Christ's name that I will do it, and therefore you must'. It means that from within my oneness with Christ these are the words I speak. If there is no oneness in Christ in what you ask, then you are not speaking in Christ's name. I think that any Christian's prayer should be such that Christ could have said it in our place.

We need no particular place to pray. The silence of a church or a room on our own is often helpful, but the beauty of the natural world can also be a great stimulus to prayer.

Christ, and so we need a lot of variety in developing that relationship.

God has given us our imagination, and we need to put it to good use in prayer. We can use variety in our posture by kneeling, sitting or standing. Sometimes it can be helpful to walk round the room, or even to walk outside praying so that we can praise the Creator as well as the Redeemer. We can use variety in our method of praying – by using a prayer list, or praying for the needs of the world after hearing the news or by reading a newspaper. We can use variety in movement by raising our hands to worship God, or holding our hands palms upwards to receive God's grace. Variety in any relationship is vital, and this is true also of our relationship with God.

Being spontaneous
Prayer thrives on spontaneity. When we pray for people through the day as situations arise, we can sense that God is continually with us, not only at the times we have set to pray. Here again, we should be free to allow our imagination to work. We can pray for people we meet in the street, or for those who look burdened. Praying before answering the door or the telephone gives us a much more positive attitude towards the person who is calling.

If Christians made prayer a reflex action to the situations they encountered, we would see much more of God's love at work in society.

Being honest before God
There should be no formulas in prayer. We do not have to begin praying by giving God praise, for example. Sometimes we try to praise God because we think we

Sustained prayer requires stamina. There is something beautiful about our early, stumbling efforts in prayer. But for a persistent and mature life of prayer we need to practise. Just as an athlete needs to train, so a Christian needs to exercise a continuing daily habit of praying.

should, but actually feel troubled about something that has happened. We should be honest and tell him what is uppermost in our minds. God knows us completely – and despite knowing us that well, he also loves us completely. We have nothing to lose by being honest with him.

Making life into prayer
God is not interested in making prayer a religious obligation which we owe to him. He does not want us to become 'religious' for short periods in the day. He longs to be involved in all that we are doing. And so we can share all our experiences with him, thankful for the gifts and situations that he has given to us.

All of life should be made into prayer. So whatever we are doing – walking, laughing, working or relaxing we can share our life with God by praising him, thanking him, talking with him and apologizing to him. Basically prayer comes down to this: sharing my life with God, so that he can share his life with me.

7
THE MAN

What kind of person was Jesus?

Down the centuries, people have pictured and thought of Jesus in many ways. He has been seen as a tragic figure, as a martyr. People have thought of him as a good, but misunderstood man, or even as somebody who did not really understand himself. Others have depicted him as a clown, and the church has added its own picture of 'Gentle Jesus, meek and mild'. So what picture of Jesus is presented to us in the Gospels?

The wrong people

Mark's Gospel tells us about an incident that happened early in Jesus' ministry, which was typical of his approach towards people.

While Jesus was having dinner at Levi's house, many tax-collectors and 'sinners' were eating with him and his disciples, for there were many who followed him.   Mark 2: 15

We are so used to hearing passages from the Bible being read in a 'respectable' church

❝ No one ever spoke the way this man does. ❞

setting that we sometimes fail to spot how shocking and controversial some of the things were that Jesus did. The church has often been very good at ignoring the unconventional side of Jesus. It has clothed him with respectability.

Jesus and 'sinners'

Mark's story would have made shocking reading for any Jew at the time. Jesus was mixing here with the most despised elements of Jewish society. To eat with a tax-collector would ruin the reputation of any Jew – let alone a Rabbi. Tax-collectors were seen as enemies of Israel because they worked for Rome. The orthodox Jews said they were unclean through their contact with non-Jews, and the common people hated them for their extortionate demands. They must have been the most unpopular figures of any Jewish town.

The passage also says that Jesus was eating with 'sinners'. This was a contemptuous term used by the Pharisees to describe those who were virtually criminals. At various times throughout his ministry Jesus associated with thieves, political agitators and prostitutes. No wonder the Pharisees were offended by his behaviour. How would we react if we heard that a popular Christian leader had been see eating and drinking with prostitutes and terrorists?

A Samaritan woman

A similar incident is related by John in his Gospel. Jesus was on his way through Samaria and at midday stopped at a well near Sychar to rest. A woman from the town came to the well to draw water, and Jesus, much to her surprise, asked her to draw some for him. This led to a conversation in which Jesus told her that he was the Messiah. The woman went back to the town and told people there about Jesus, with the result that many of them began to believe in Jesus.

Barriers in Jewish society

This conversation between Jesus and the Samaritan woman shows how far Jesus was prepared to break the social rules of his time to meet people's needs. There were a number of prejudices which should have prevented this conversation from taking place at all. There was a prejudice against women, as there still is in many parts of the world. Jewish teachers warned against speaking to a woman in public, and one writer even said, 'Let no one talk with a woman in the street, no, not with his own wife.'

A team of people at St George's Crypt in Leeds, England, work to help homeless people. Jack, one of the team, is here mending clothes given by people from the town. His aim is that his customers need never be ashamed of their dress. This high value set on the practical side of our lives is a true reflection of Jesus' ministry.

This was why the woman was so shocked when Jesus began talking with her at the well.

Then there were racial tensions between the Jews and the Samaritans. The Jews regarded the Samaritans as a mixed race, as they had originally been Jews, but had intermarried with other races.

There was also a religious problem in that the Samaritans refused to worship in the Jerusalem Temple, which the Jews believed was essential to the true worship of God. Added to this was a political tension. Two hundred years earlier the Samaritans had aided the Syrians in a war against the Jews.

JESUS AND THE SAMARITAN WOMAN

A most revealing story from John's Gospel:

In Samaria, Jesus came to a town named Sychar, which was not far from the field that Jacob had given to his son Joseph. Jacob's well was there, and Jesus, tired out by the journey, sat down by the well. It was about noon.

A Samaritan woman came to draw some water, and Jesus said to her, 'Give me a drink of water.' (His disciples had gone into town to buy food.) The woman answered, 'You are a Jew, and I am a Samaritan — so how can you ask me for a drink?' (Jews will not use the same cups and bowls that Samaritans use.) Jesus answered, 'If only you knew what God gives and who it is that is asking you for a drink, you would ask him, and he would give you life-giving water.

'Sir', the woman said, 'you haven't got a bucket, and the well is deep. Where would you get that life-giving water? It was our ancestor Jacob who gave us this well; he and his sons

and his flocks all drank from it. You don't claim to be greater than Jacob, do you?' Jesus answered, 'Whoever drinks this water will be thirsty again, but whoever drinks the water that I will give him will never be thirsty again. The water that I will give him will become in him a spring which will provide him with life-giving water and give him eternal life.'

'Sir,' the woman said, 'give me that water! Then I will never be thirsty again, nor will I have to come here to draw water.' 'Go and call your husband,' Jesus told her, 'and come back.' 'I haven't got a husband,' she answered. Jesus replied, 'You are right when you say you haven't got a husband. You have been married to five men, and the man you live with now is not really your husband. You have told me the truth.'

'I see you are a prophet, sir,' the woman said. 'My Samaritan ancestors worshipped God on this mountain, but you Jews say that Jerusalem is the place

where we should worship God.' Jesus said to her, 'Believe me, woman, the time will come when people will not worship the Father either on this mountain or in Jerusalem. You Samaritans do not really know whom you worship; but we Jews know whom we worship, because it is from the Jews that salvation comes. But the time is coming and is already here, when by the power of God's Spirit people will worship the Father as he really is, offering him the true worship that he wants. God is Spirit, and only by the power of his Spirit can people worship him as he really is.'

The woman said to him, 'I know that the Messiah will come, and when he comes, he will tell us everything.' Jesus answered, 'I am he, I who am talking with you.'
John 4:5-26

So, in talking with this woman, Jesus cut across many of the prejudices current in his time: sexual, racial, religious and political. Many of his encounters with people show him willing to disregard convention where he felt it was necessary.

Was Jesus unconventional for the sake of it?

Some people may feel that Jesus was simply a natural nonconformist, who enjoyed being different just for the sake of it. But the Gospel accounts make it obvious that, when Jesus said or did something shocking, it was always for a greater purpose.

When Jesus was unconventional, it was always because some prejudice stood in the way of his helping someone in need. And when that happened, Jesus' priority was to show God's love. He was different not merely because he acted differently, but because his compassion for people refused to be limited by the rules and regulations of his time.

The anger of Jesus

Jesus was a man with very strong feelings. When he saw injustices carried out against the weak in society he became angry with leaders who abused their positions of authority. Towards

Jesus once said, 'I am among you as one who serves.' He was quick to see people's deepest needs and had the power and the love to meet them.

the end of his life, he said of the Pharisees:

They tie on to people's backs loads that are heavy and hard to carry, yet they aren't willing even to lift a finger to help them carry those loads.   Matthew 23: 4

His outspoken attacks on the scribes and Pharisees made him a very unpopular figure with the Jewish establishment in Jerusalem.

The patience of Jesus
Yet Jesus did not spend all his time breaking conventions and throwing merchants out of the Temple in anger. He always had time for the ordinary people and he was patient with their

difficulties in understanding who he was. Most of his healing miracles were worked for people who were poor and unknown. He preached the message of God's kingdom not to some small elite, but to the large crowds who followed him. His main concern was that the common, working people should experience and understand God's good news.

The humour of Jesus
Jesus spoke in parables partly so that the people could easily understand his message. And although none of the Gospel writers tell us that Jesus laughed, there are obvious elements of humour in many of his sayings. He clearly intended his audience to laugh as they took in the point he was making.

A popular form of humour in Jesus' time was exaggeration, and Jesus used this to show how ridiculous sin is. After a conversation with a rich man, Jesus once observed,

It is much harder for a rich person to enter the kingdom of God than for a camel to go through the eye of a needle.
Luke 18: 25

In Jewish culture, the camel was regarded as the largest animal in creation.

'I am the way,' said Jesus. 'No one comes to the Father except by me.' If we aim to know God, Jesus shows us what he is like and takes away the barriers to knowing him.

The man from the north country
The humanity and strength of
Jesus come across clearly in the
Gospel accounts. He spoke the
language of the country people
he lived with, filling his stories
with the details of agricultural
life, and with humour. He
encouraged the poor and
powerless to believe that God
cared for them and valued their
faith. He was not afraid to attack
hypocrisy and evil wherever he
met it. Jesus was a unique
personality in Palestine and it is
no wonder that almost everywhere he went he attracted large
crowds of people.

Who did Jesus say he was?

Because of his unconventional behaviour, Jesus attracted
two kinds of attention: those who followed him, and those
who plotted to kill him. People could not make up their
minds about who he was, but everybody was talking
about him. He finally asked his disciples a question: 'Who
do the crowds say I am?'

They replied, '*Some say John the Baptist; others say
Elijah; and still others, that one of the prophets of long
ago has come back to life.' 'But what about you?' he
asked. 'Who do you say I am?' Peter answered, 'The
Christ of God.'*

The authority of Jesus
For a long time, the identity of
Jesus had been puzzling his
disciples. When he revisited
Nazareth and spoke in the
synagogue on the Sabbath, the
local people were amazed at his
words and found it hard to
believe that he was the same
carpenter who had worked in
their village. Mark tells us about
their astonishment:

'Where did he get all this?' they
asked. 'What wisdom is this that
has been given him? How does he
perform miracles? Isn't he the
carpenter...?'   Mark 6: 2, 3

Other Rabbis quoted the
interpretations of great Jewish
teachers from the past, but Jesus
refused to do so. Instead, he
taught on the strength of his own
authority. On one occasion he
said,

You have heard that it was said,
'An eye for an eye, and a tooth for
a tooth.' But now I tell you: do
not take revenge on someone
who wrongs you.   Matthew 5: 38, 39

Who was this person who quoted himself as an authority?

Fulfilled prophecy
There were times when Jesus claimed that he was fulfilling what the prophets had written about in the Old Testament. To his Jewish listeners this would imply that God was finally doing through Jesus what he had promised centuries earlier. Near the beginning of his ministry, in the synagogue at Nazareth, Jesus read a passage from the prophet Isaiah. When he had finished, he said,

This passage of scripture has come true today, as you heard it being read.
Luke 4: 21

Jesus obviously believed that he was quite different from any other teacher, and even the people began to compare him with some of the great figures in their history, such as Moses and Elijah.

Forgiving sins
More boldly still, Jesus told people that their sins were forgiven. At one time, when a paralysed man was brought to him for healing, Jesus first said to him, 'Friend, your sins are forgiven'. The Pharisees and teachers of the law who were sitting watching were horrified, and rightly observed, 'Who can forgive sins but God alone?' Jesus went on to heal the man, showing that he had the power to forgive people their sins. Again Jesus' behaviour caused people to ask questions about his identity. When Jesus told an immoral woman that her sins were forgiven, the onlookers asked, 'Who is this who even forgives sins?'

Judging all people
The favourite name Jesus gave to himself was 'the Son of man'. He once told his disciples a parable in which the Son of man would send out his angels to execute God's judgement on the earth. So who was Jesus implying that he was? At this point in his ministry, Jesus would not specifically say. In fact, he deliberately avoided the subject, as he knew people would misunderstand him.

❝ **Jesus explained to them what was said about himself in all the Scriptures. ❞**

The Messiah
When at last Jesus asked the disciples who they thought he was, Peter said that he was the Messiah (or 'Christ', which is Greek for Messiah). Jesus did not deny this, but went on to correct their idea of what the Messiah would do. The disciples probably thought that as the Messiah Jesus would become the political deliverer of Israel, driving the Romans out of the

country. They certainly must have thought he would soon become a powerful and kingly figure, or else James and John would not have asked him,

When you sit on your throne in your glorious kingdom, we want you to let us sit with you, one at your right and one at your left.
Mark 10: 37

But Jesus' words about his role as Messiah were quite the opposite of what they might have expected. He said,

The Son of man must suffer many things and be rejected by the elders, chief priests and teachers of the law, and he must be killed and on the third day be raised to life.   Luke 9: 22

The disciples were totally unprepared for anything like this. They were bewildered and confused.

John's view

John's Gospel gave us the same answer as Matthew, Mark and Luke to the question of who Jesus was, but he put it even more strongly. The first three Gospels only hint at Jesus' identity, but John records words of Jesus in which he openly declares himself. In John, Jesus says that he is the only way to God, and that he and God the Father are one. John draws the conclusion

JESUS TELLS US WHO HE IS

John's Gospel gives us sections of teaching that we do not find in any of the other three Gospels. John underlines his picture of Jesus with a series of sayings, all of which begin with the words, 'I am'. These sayings sum up who Jesus was and what he had come to do:

I am the bread of life. He who comes to me will never go hungry, and he who believes in me will never be thirsty.

I am the light of the world. Whoever follows me will never walk in darkness, but will have the light of life.

I am the gate for the sheep. All who ever came before me were thieves and robbers, but the sheep did not listen to them. I am the gate; whoever enters through me will be saved. He will come in and go out, and find pasture.

I am the good shepherd; I know my sheep and my sheep know me — just as the Father knows me and I know the Father — and I lay down my life for the sheep.

I am the resurrection and the life. He who believes in me will live, even though he dies; and whoever lives and believes in me will never die.

I am the way and the truth and the life. No one comes to the Father except through me.

I am the vine; you are the branches. If a man remains in me and I in him, he will bear much fruit; apart from me you can do nothing.

that is implicit in the accounts of Jesus' words and actions in Matthew, Mark and Luke – that Jesus was a man, but he was also the Son of God.

Reactions to Jesus' words

One way we can be sure that this is really what Jesus was saying is by looking at the reaction of the orthodox Jews who heard his words. His listeners were often shocked by what he said, but their reaction went beyond that. To say the sort of things Jesus was saying if it was not true was nothing short of blasphemy – and this is exactly what Jesus was accused of. At other times the crowd even picked up stones to kill Jesus for saying such things. It seems that the words of Jesus were so strong that people either had to believe in him or to condemn him. Jesus left them with no other choice.

Who is Jesus?

We cannot dispute that Jesus said he was the Son of God. But just as people in the time of Jesus were free to decide for themselves whether what he was saying was true, so are we today. The writers of the four Gospels wrote to challenge their first-century readers about this question, and it is a challenge they make to their twentieth-century readers as well.

Just another religious teacher?

Many people like to think of Jesus as a great religious teacher, the founder of one of the world religions. They see him as a figure on the same sort of level as the Buddha or Muhammad. Can we really see Jesus in those terms, when we have examined what he had to say about himself? What Jesus said about his identity is, to say the least, extraordinary. There is no equivalent in any of the world religions. In fact, we find quite the opposite when we consider Buddha and Muhammad.

Buddha and Muhammad

Far from making any startling statements about himself, Buddha directed attention away from himself, so that his disciples would not be distracted in their search for release from earthly sensations and pleasures. He certainly did not see himself or any other teacher as essential to this search.

Similarly, Muhammad, the founder of Islam, pointed away from himself. Very little is said about him in the Qur'an. He insisted that he was only a man without any supernatural powers beyond receiving the Qur'an from the hands of Allah. Even today, orthodox Islam regards any form of worship addressed to Muhammad as worse than heresy.

World religion contest?

Clearly Jesus was quite different from these two great religious figures, in that he had a great deal to say about himself. Where Muslim and Buddhist belief rest

Islam has certain points of contact with Christianity. But at a vital point is is different: the way people come to know God. For Muslims this is through the Qur'an; for Christians entirely through Jesus Christ. Jesus claimed to be the full revelation of God.

upon the *teaching* of Muhammad and Buddha, Christian belief centres on the *person* of Jesus. Without Jesus Christ, the Christian faith would not exist.

To compare religions in this way is unpopular today. One writer has said that to do this is rather like holding a beauty contest of world religions, where we decide which one we like best. So should we talk about religions in this way?

Searching for the truth
If we are looking for the truth, we are entitled to weigh up the evidence for ourselves. And the fact is that, when we listen to what Jesus said about himself,

FROM HINDUISM TO CHRISTIANITY

Nishi Sharma is a producer of audio visual materials. For the past five years Nishi has lived in Surrey, England. He is married with children. Nishi was asked how his spiritual understanding has developed:

What first attracted you to Christianity?
I think I was attracted towards Christians whom I met. I lived in India for twenty-four years, and I never met a Christian. When I went to the Western state of Nigeria, I met some Nigerian Christians, and I remember in one meeting there was a Nigerian Christian who was preaching. I do not remember what he said, but the thing that attracted me towards the Christian faith was that he was speaking from conviction. He seemed to know God in a personal way. I had met lots of Hindu gurus and I found that there was something missing in their lives. There was a lack of conviction in their lives.

So how does Jesus differ from the Hindu gods you were brought up to believe in?
Well, in Hinduism there are about 36,000 gods, so it depends on which god you are talking about. We had some family gods, and I found that their life was very different from the life of Jesus. Hindu gods often pointed out the way man should go, but they never accompanied anybody. They indicated what sort of morality man should have, but they never gave any strength to cope with that standard which is set before us. I also found the Hindu gods very impersonal — I have a special relationship with Jesus now which I never had with any gods in Hinduism.

What is it that most impresses you about Jesus?
I think the fact that God became man and lived among us, and lived a sinless life, is something which I find very challenging. There are many Hindu gods who have incarnated, but none of them lived a sinless life, and nobody died for the sins of other people. Also the humility of Jesus. In our society, humility does not play a great part. As people we do not like being humiliated at all; we always defend ourselves and we do not like being insulted in any way. So when I read about Jesus, that people spat on him and he did not defend himself, I find that quite a revolutionary thing. I think he rode on a donkey when he went to Jerusalem. In the Indian culture, a donkey is a very despised animal — it is used by washermen to carry clothes. So I found this quite hard to accept. He could have used a horse, so why did he use a donkey? I was a bit embarrassed about it as well. I thought that when I told my parents, or other friends who were Hindus, they would really laugh about it. Why did he ride on a donkey? But now I find that donkey symbolizes his humility, and that was one thing that really stood out for me.

we hear things that no one in their right mind would dream of saying unless they were true.

What would our reaction be if

> 66 **Come to me, all you who are weary and burdened, and I will give you rest.** 99

somebody said to us: 'Do you want to know what God is like? Look at me! Do you want to know God yourself? I am the only person who can lead you to him. I have the right to forgive all your sins. God has given me authority over all the powers of this world. One day I will judge all the people who have ever lived, and your destiny will depend entirely on your response to me.' Such a person would obviously be saying things that were quite different from any other religious teacher. And these are the kind of things that we are told Jesus said.

Of course, we might think that Jesus was mad, or a confidence trickster. But when we look at the way Jesus lived – healing and caring for the sick and the unknown – and at the quality and wisdom of his teaching, it is difficult to come to the conclusion that he was evil or insane.

Jesus' accepting love reached out to people whom the society of his time rejected. The Gospels tell us of Mary Magdalene and of the woman of Samaria. Spurned by the respectable, they found new life in him.

'A good man'

Frequently, people are happy to think of Jesus as a good man, and to leave it at that. But, if Jesus really was only a good *man*, why did he claim to be equal with God? Would a good man do such a thing?

A Christian writer, C.S. Lewis, once summed up the alternatives we have in responding to Jesus' claims for himself: 'I am trying here to prevent anyone saying the really foolish thing that

66 I am in the Father and the Father is in me. 99

people often say about him: "I'm ready to accept Jesus as a moral teacher, but I don't accept His claim to be God." That is the one thing we must not say. A man who was merely a man and said the sort of things Jesus said would not be a great moral teacher. He would either be a lunatic – on a level with the man who says he is a poached egg – or else he would be the Devil of Hell. You must make your choice. Either this man was, and is, the Son of God: or else a madman or' something worse.'

'Anyone can claim to be God'
The list of people who have

David Watson and Tina Heath chat in the television studio. Television takes instant opinion to millions, but Jesus' teaching spread entirely by word of mouth. Yet his influence has reached round the world and across the centuries.

Jesus got a reputation for mixing with people respectable society deplored. In fact the deeper people's need, the more strongly Jesus was drawn to them.

claimed to be God is a long one, so Jesus is by no means unique in that sense. The uniqueness of Jesus lies in the fact that the way he lived gives us good reason to believe what he said was true. Many of those who have said that they are God have in time been shown up as rogues or madmen. The evidence of the way they lived did not support their claims.

What makes Jesus different is that he not only said these things, but also showed compassion, healed the sick, did not play to the crowd but had time for the unnoticed, died for the sake of others, and was raised from the dead. The sheer scope of Jesus' character and work supports his words in a way that we see in no other human life.

The challenge of Jesus

Early on in his ministry, Jesus and his disciples crossed over the Sea of Galilee after a particularly tiring day. Jesus fell asleep in the boat, and remained

sleeping while a storm blew up. The disciples became terrified because of the strength of the storm and woke Jesus, who stilled the storm, saying, 'Quiet! Be still!' The response of the disciples was to say to each other, 'Who is this? Even the wind and the waves obey him!'

Today, as in his own day, Jesus presents us with the problem of how we should think about him. The Gospel accounts give us a picture of Jesus as a man unusual in his own time, challenging the conventions that tried to prevent him from reaching out to people. But clearly his unusual qualities extended beyond that. It is easier for us to admire his bold overturning of convention than it is seriously to look at the astonishing things he said about himself. Because when we consider who he said he was, we can no longer simply admire him from a distance. (Jesus never wanted admirers, he wanted followers.) He asks us to choose whether we will ignore who he really was, or whether we will accept him as God, and follow him.

8
OPPOSITION

Why was Jesus arrested?

For some time the authorities had been looking for the right moment to arrest and silence Jesus. When he arrived in Jerusalem for the Passover celebrations, they began actively to plan a way to engineer his death. But, this was not as easy as it seemed. Luke tells us about the dilemma of the authorities: *'Every day Jesus taught in the Temple. The chief priests, the teachers of the Law, and the leaders of the people wanted to kill him, but they could not find a way to do it, because all the people kept listening to him, not wanting to miss a single word.'*

To arrest Jesus in broad daylight, while he was teaching in the Temple, would undoubtedly have provoked a riot. But the ideal opportunity to seize Jesus came when one of his own followers, Judas, offered to inform the leaders of Jesus' whereabouts at night. All four Gospel accounts show us that there was a considerable amount of discussion and plotting behind closed doors about how to get rid of Jesus. Why were they so determined to kill him?

Jesus was popular
During his life, Jesus had enjoyed great popularity among the people. Quite apart from his willingness to heal those who were ill, he was also popular for the authority of his words, and because people hoped he was the Messiah who would change the fortunes of Israel.

The excitement about Jesus reached a climax on the day he entered Jerusalem during the final week of his life.

They brought the colt to Jesus, threw their cloaks on the colt and put Jesus on it. As he went along, people spread their cloaks on the road. When he came near the place where the road goes down the Mount of Olives, the whole crowd of disciples began joyfully to praise God in loud voices for all the miracles they had seen: 'Blessed is the king who comes in the name of the Lord!' 'Peace in heaven and glory in the highest!' Some of the Pharisees in the crowd said to Jesus, 'Teacher, rebuke your disciples!' 'I tell you,' he replied, 'if they keep quiet, the stones will cry out.' Luke 19: 35 – 40

But only four days after these scenes of excitement, a crowd was standing outside the Roman governor's headquarters shouting for his death. How was it possible for Jesus' popularity to disappear so quickly?

Jesus was orthodox
Jesus was deeply committed to the Old Testament scriptures, as the Jewish authorities were. His teaching pointed the people back to the need for genuine devotion to God, an aim shared by the religious parties of his day. And Jesus made it clear that he did not intend his teaching to replace the Old Testament teaching:

Do not think that I have come to do away with the Law of Moses and the teachings of the prophets. I have not come to do away with them, but to make their teachings come true.
Matthew 5: 17

Jesus' chief opponents were the religious leaders of his time. There is a danger for all religious people to be so wedded to details of church practice that they fail to accept Jesus' way of freedom.

Why then should all the religious parties unite to destroy him?

Jesus did not act as a political Messiah

Jesus would not openly refer to himself as the Messiah, because he knew that this would be misunderstood as a political claim. Often in the Gospels we read how he told people not to talk of him in this way. He preferred to call himself 'the Son of man', which did not have the political overtones of 'Messiah'.

Despite the careful way in which Jesus distanced himself from a political role, the crowds still wanted to pin the Messiah label on him. The Gospels all record incidents in which Jesus was followed out into lonely places by enormous crowds of people – once at least there were 5,000 men. These crowds did not form only because people were astonished at the beauty and depth of Jesus' teaching. They also hoped to hear Jesus declare himself politically.

After Jesus had miraculously provided food for such a crowd, John's Gospel records some significant words:

Jesus knew that they were about to come and seize him in order to make him king by force; so he went off again to the hills by himself. John 6: 15

Jesus consistently refused these attempts to make him a king, and he would not organize resistance to the Roman auth-orities or teach against them. So why should the Jerusalem leaders see him as a threat to the political status quo?

Blasphemy

There were many reasons why the authorities felt Jesus to be a threat, and their opposition to him went back to the very beginnings of his ministry. On a number of occasions, Jesus was accused of saying things that amounted to blasphemy. Once, previously, when Jesus was in Jerusalem, a crowd picked up stones to kill him, saying,

We do not want to stone you because of any good deeds, but because of your blasphemy! You are only a man, but you are trying to make yourself God!
John 10: 33

The company Jesus kept

Another scandal about Jesus was that he associated with people no devout Jew would even speak to. He not only spoke with them, but he also accepted their hospitality, attended their parties and ate and drank with them. This brought him into collision with the convictions of groups such as the Pharisees.

The Sabbath

The Pharisees made it their aim in life to teach people how to obey God's Law as it had been given in the Old Testament. To do this they provided detailed interpretations of the Law, covering the most minute details of human behaviour. They determined that there were thirty-nine main types of activity that were prohibited on the Sabbath day. Some of their interpretations of the Law meant that they were not allowed to trim their nails or search for fleas in their clothes on the Sabbath!

Jesus had no time for such interpretations of the Old Testament. In the early days of his ministry, the Pharisees caught Jesus' disciples picking ears of corn for food on the

❝ This man welcomes outcasts and even eats with them! ❞

Sabbath. But, far from apologizing for their behaviour, Jesus defended them and attacked the views of the Pharisees. Another time, when Jesus actually healed on the Sabbath, we are told for the first time that the Pharisees began to plot to kill him.

'Sons of hell'
When Jesus arrived in Jerusalem, he had a series of confrontations with the religious leaders, in which he publicly humiliated them for their lack of love for the people and for God. Jesus did not draw back from using the most sarcastic language in ridiculing his opponents:

How terrible for you, teachers of the Law and Pharisees! You hypocrites! You sail the seas and cross whole countries to win one convert; and when you succeed, you make him twice as deserving of going to hell as you yourselves are! Matthew 23: 15

We are told that at times Jesus' attacks on the religious leaders humiliated them, much to the delight of the crowd. Such humiliation can only have provoked a desire for revenge.

The Sadducees
Although Christians have traditionally thought of the Pharisees as the ones responsible for Jesus' death, the Sanhedrin (or Jewish council), which worked so hard to secure a death sentence, was largely made up of the aristocratic Sadducees. The Pharisees and the Sadducees had long been enemies, but Jesus managed to unite the two groups in opposition to himself.

The Sadducees were very concerned that no one should upset the working arrangement they had built up with the Romans. Although Jesus would not come out into the open politically, he did make some remarks about the future of the Jewish nation that the Sadducees saw as dangerous. He said that Israel was about to be judged by God, that Jerusalem would be destroyed, and that there was no hope for the nation politically. Because of the popularity of Jesus, such words could not be allowed to pass without taking action against him.

How was Jesus opposed?
In the early days, Jesus' opponents confined themselves to verbal attacks. But, as his later preaching seems to have taken place entirely out of doors, it looks as though Jesus was forbidden to speak any longer inside the synagogues. It was only as his reputation grew, and as he became a political threat, that the plotting against him became serious and determined. Finally, Jesus was arrested in a quiet valley outside Jerusalem at night.

What charges were brought against Jesus?

Once Jesus had been arrested, the authorities had to make sure that they could find him guilty of a charge that would secure the death penalty. However, it was not enough for them to satisfy themselves on this point and convict him under Jewish law. They also had the more difficult task of convincing the Romans.

The religious trials
The enemies of Jesus brought a religious charge against him before the Jewish court. Their accusation was that he was guilty of blasphemy – a crime punishable by death under Jewish law. Jesus appeared before the Sanhedrin, which was the highest court of the Jews, and they had the task of finding him guilty on the evidence of two witnesses in agreement with each other. The Old Testament law clearly stated:

On the testimony of two or three witnesses a man shall be put to death, but no one shall be put to death on the testimony of only one witness. Deuteronomy 17: 6

But, the trial did not go as smoothly as they had hoped. The witnesses gave conflicting evidence against Jesus and their testimony was disqualified. And Jesus himself refused to answer any of their questions about what he had taught.

'Tell us if you are the Messiah!'
Finally, the High Priest himself asked Jesus a question under oath: was Jesus the Messiah? Jesus responded with the guarded reply, 'So you say'. Probably Jesus was saying something like: 'Yes, I am the Messiah, but not in the sense that you understand the word.' This reply left the Sanhedrin in no doubt that Jesus was guilty of

blasphemy, as charged.

The political trial

The Jews were not allowed to put anyone to death themselves without the authority of the Romans. So they took Jesus to the Procurator of Judea, who at that time was Pontius Pilate. According to two Jewish writers

Jesus was unjustly tried: the witnesses did not agree. Yet the verdict was guilty, because the issues went beyond factual truth. This was a confrontation between two radically different approaches to what God requires of us.

of the period, Philo and Josephus, Pontius Pilate was an obstinate, cruel, inflexible and oppressive man. The portrait painted of him by the Gospel writers highlights a fundamental weakness beneath all this, as he was swayed by the voice of the crowd. He was in charge of all the Roman troops stationed in Judea, and had the power to reverse or to ratify any sentence passed by the Jewish Sanhedrin.

The leaders of the Sanhedrin knew that Pilate would not be the least interested in any obscure

religious charge against Jesus. So when they brought Jesus before Pilate, they accused him of crimes which had not even been mentioned in the earlier trials.

Luke tells us that the three political charges brought against Jesus were revolutionary activity, inciting the people not to pay the Roman taxes and claiming to be a king. The Sanhedrin clearly had their own definition of the word 'Messiah', and now that Jesus had admitted to the title, they used its political connotations to the full.

Pilate's indecision

On examining Jesus for himself, Pilate could not agree that Jesus had claimed these things. There followed a series of arguments between Pilate and the Jewish authorities, which only seemed to make Pilate more convinced of Jesus' innocence.

The Gospels suggest that Pilate was a weak man, who quickly found out that Jesus was not guilty, but who feared bad reports reaching the Emperor about another disturbance in Judea. Pilate had provoked the Jews to violence on a number of previous occasions through his own insensitivity to their beliefs and customs. The mob that had gathered outside Pilate's residence played skilfully on Pilate's fear:

'If you set him free,' they shouted, 'you are not the Emperor's friend! Anyone who claims to be a king is a rebel against the Emperor!'
John 19: 12

So Pilate attempted to evade his responsibility by making other people decide what should be done with Jesus. He sent him to Herod, because Jesus as a Galilean came under Herod's jurisdiction. But after questioning him, and receiving only silence for reply, Herod would not take the accusations against Jesus seriously. He regarded Jesus as an object of mockery rather than as worthy of death. So Pilate had Jesus flogged, hoping that this limited punishment would pacify the crowd. When this too failed, he offered to grant Jesus clemency, leaving the crowd with the responsibility to decide between Jesus and the criminal Barabbas.

Sentenced to death

All these evasions of responsibility meant that the

❝ What crime has this man committed? ❞

crowd was the deciding factor in the whole affair. And the crowd were determined to stop at nothing short of Jesus' death. So Jesus was sentenced to death, not because he was found to be guilty, but because of the hatred of the authorities and their desire to see him killed.

How is Jesus opposed today?

We cannot see the opposition Jesus faced as some local affair. Jesus was arrested and condemned not just because of the religious and political circumstances of the time, but also because he stood firmly for goodness and justice. He was so committed to these qualities that he immediately showed up the corrupt and oppressive for what they were.

Jesus told his disciples that the opposition he experienced would be their experience too. They also would be attacked for their commitment to the goodness of God. So what did Jesus say about the way his followers should regard persecution?

'Take up the cross'

Jesus talked about the consequence of following him in the worst possible terms: carrying a cross. One who carried a cross knew that ahead lay ridicule, pain and death. So the opposition Christians must face is not an accident, it is a direct result of following Jesus.

This does not mean that Christians should look for opposition, or go out of their way to create it by being unreasonable, obnoxious or unkind. Jesus talked about being persecuted *for following him*, and for no other reason.

'Follow me'

Christians have often thought of following Jesus Christ in purely personal terms: overcoming personal sins and learning to pray and become familiar with the Bible. All these things are important, but it means more than this.

Jesus drew fire from his enemies because of his determination to bring God's love to the working people, even to those who were despised. He stirred up trouble for himself by his outspoken attacks on the oppressive behaviour of those who were supposed to be religious leaders. He attacked them as 'blind guides', who led the people into great misery. Jesus lived out the goodness and justice of God in an evil and unjust society – and Christians are called to do the same.

Unfortunately, Christians have often avoided following Jesus in that way. We fail to follow the Jesus who rocked the boat and put people's backs up over the real abuses in society. Many

Christians are so concerned not to give offence nor to be seen as in any way revolutionary, that they fail to be true disciples of Jesus. There are real abuses in the world. If we do not feel the need for those abuses to be attacked as strongly as Jesus attacked the shortcomings of the Pharisees, we are stopping short of following Jesus properly.

The kingdom of God

Jesus spoke about the kingdom of God as God's alternative to the way that the rest of the world lives. In his time, as in ours, people felt free to live according

LOVE FOR PERSECUTORS

Jesus spoke about loving our enemies and praying for those who attack us. Festo Kivengere, an Anglican bishop in Uganda, faced the problem of persecution under Idi Amin's regime. On 16 February, 1977 Archbishop Janani Luwum was murdered by the security forces. Bishop Festo, the author of a book I Love Idi Amin, described his feelings on hearing the news of the Archbishop's death:

Early in the morning the paper came with the headline that the Archbishop and the two cabinet ministers had died in a car accident between the place of arrest and another place for questioning. And then the whole country was paralysed by that terrible news. And yet, on Sunday, four days after his death, St Paul's Cathedral in Kampala was crowded out with nearly 5,000 worshippers: students and young people who walked to church singing. That singing was of course very difficult because it was singing with tears and with joy. And those who were present tell me that it was just like being in heaven.

And the news went back to Amin: the Christians were rejoicing, singing — and he just could not make sense out of the thing. I think this is where the secret lies really, that Christians shine better when they are exposed to pressure. I do not think that is extraordinary for Uganda; I think that it is the nature of our faith. For, you see, the faith was not born in seclusion. Our faith was born outside the city in absolute violence on the cross, and a faith born that way never succumbs.

The title of my book, *I love Idi Amin*, of course can give the wrong impression, as if it were just one of those little Christian cliches. But in fact it came out of a press conference when I arrived in the United States as an exiled bishop. The Amin thing was still very hard, and I faced some tough questions. One black man said to me, 'Why is it that you hesitate to condemn Amin — a terrible man? Don't confuse us, condemn him!' Then I said, by the help of the Holy Spirit, 'My ministry is not the ministry of condemnation. My ministry is the ministry of reconciliation.'

And then he said, 'Supposing I brought Amin and made him stand there in front of you and I gave you a pistol. Tell me, what would you do with that pistol?' That was a little bit tough, but I said to him, 'Look, I would hand over the gun to Amin, saying, "Take your weapon, it belongs to you. I've never used it, I don't believe in it. My only weapon is love."' I love Idi Amin because by not loving him my protest would have failed.

to socially acceptable standards: taking revenge on those who wronged them; despising the outcasts of society; making the

66 **Anyone who does not carry his cross and follow me cannot be my disciple.** **99**

accumulation of personal wealth an aim in life. Jesus rejected these standards of behaviour and told his followers to love in a

Festo Kivengere, a bishop in the Ugandan church, belongs to a church which has been through the fire. Both in their confrontations with President Amin's regime and in their efforts to bring reconciliation since then, Christians have often been in the firing line.

radically different way. Once he said,

You know that the men who are considered rulers of the heathen have power over them, and the leaders have complete authority. This, however, is not the way it is among you. If one of you wants to be great, he must be the servant of the rest; and if one of you wants to be first, he must be the slave of all. Mark 10: 42 – 44

Those who live in the kingdom of God challenge the world by their behaviour, and also by their opposition to injustice. Sadly, the church has often failed to follow Jesus in this way. We have allowed wrong attitudes,

prevalent in society, to become the norm within the church. So there has been racial prejudice, for example, or prejudice based on income or reputation. We have become preoccupied with raising our standards of living, ignoring the needs of the poor. These are attitudes we need to turn from in the church today. The world should look at us and see that we are different. We are meant to be God's alternative society.

These Orthodox Christians worshipping in Siberia have not accepted their state's atheistic position. A whole range of Christian witness is carried on in the Soviet Union, though sometimes the force of the law comes down on the Christians.

Happy are the persecuted!
Jesus once spoke some bewildering words to his disciples:

Happy are you when people insult you and persecute you and tell all kinds of evil lies against you because you are my followers. Be happy and glad, for a great reward is kept for you in heaven. This is how the prophets who lived before you were persecuted. Matthew 5: 11, 12

When the church begins to live as God's alternative society and to challenge the injustices in society, it will begin to feel the pressure of opposition. This is why Jesus said that his disciples

OSCAR ROMERO

Oscar Romero was the Archbishop of San Salvador. He was cynically appointed to this post by the military government of El Salvador, who thought he would cause them little trouble because of his shy, conservative nature. But within four weeks of assuming office he came into conflict with the authorities. A peaceful protest against the 'fixing' of the presidential elections in 1977 was brutally broken up by the police. They fired directly into the crowd to disperse the demonstration; many were killed. Romero protested vigorously against this.

Soon after this, a close friend of Romero's, a Jesuit priest working among the very poor, was murdered by right-wing forces. Romero was transformed. He began increasingly to speak out against violence, whether by government forces or by the opposing left-wing groups. He also attacked the government for its brutal oppression of the peasants of El Salvador. As a result, he became a central figure in his country, and the weekly radio broadcast of his sermons became a feature of national life. Both left- and right-wing groups plotted to take his life.

On 24 March 1980, Romero celebrated mass in San Salvador. As he raised the cup above his head he said, 'May Christ's sacrifice give us the courage to offer our own bodies for justice and peace.' At that very moment he was shot dead by an assassin.

should be happy at opposition –
not because they derived some
perverse pleasure from being
insulted, but because persecution

66 **If they persecuted me, they
will persecute you too.** **99**

showed they were doing what
God wanted of them.

Opposition should therefore not
come as a shock to Jesus'
followers, because he said this
would happen. Not everyone who
is a true disciple of Jesus Christ
will experience the same
intensity of opposition that he
did, but many in today's world do
face these kinds of pressure.

Love your enemies

**You have heard that it was said,
'Love your neighbour and hate
your enemy.' But I tell you: Love
your enemies and pray for those
who persecute you, that you may
be sons of your Father in
heaven.** Matthew 5: 43 – 45

Again Jesus asked his followers
not to give in to their natural, and
evil, desires when they went
through extremes of opposition.

*The example of Martin Luther King Jr
shows that a stand for love and justice can
provoke a powerful reaction of anger. His
peaceful methods of protest were
sometimes met with explosive violence and
in the end he was killed.*

MARTIN LUTHER KING

Martin Luther King Jr was a
man who paid the full price
for his commitment to Jesus
and to justice. He
campaigned in the
southern United States
against the oppression and
segregation of black
Americans by the white
community. His approach
combined concern for
justice and for peace. He
refused to preach
comfortable words to
reconcile black people to
their situation. And he
rejected the use of violence
by the black community in
striving for its goals. This
enraged his white
opponents, because his
peaceful approach,
coupled with love for his
enemies, defeated them on
moral grounds alone.

In 1963, during a series of
demonstrations against
segregation in Birmingham,
Alabama, the peaceful
demonstrators were
attacked by police with fire
hoses, dogs and clubs.
Martin Luther King and
3,000 others were gaoled.
On other occasions his
house was burned, he
received death threats, and
was assaulted by white
reactionaries. Finally, in
April 1968, while organizing
protests in Memphis,
Tennessee, he was
assassinated on the balcony
of his hotel.

Jesus said, 'Remember the
words I spoke to you: "No
servant is greater than his
master." If they persecuted
me, they will persecute you
also.'

On a human level, if someone is unfriendly towards us, we do not speak to them; if they insult us, we return the insult; if they harm us, our thoughts turn to how we can pay them back.

Jesus calls us to deny ourselves that kind of behaviour, and that is very difficult, as it means struggling against our own instincts. But still we should not hold back from criticizing those who oppress and mislead others, as long as we also show the love of God in the way we act personally towards the oppressors. It was Jesus who called the Pharisees 'hypocrites', but who also said while suffering on the cross,

'Father, forgive them, for they do not know what they are doing.'
Luke 23: 34

9
CRUCIFIXION

Why is the cross central to Christianity?

Reading the accounts of Jesus' crucifixion, it is obvious how much Jesus suffered. He was betrayed and deserted by his closest friends, humilated, beaten and put to death in the most horrible way. But despite all this, the crucifixion was quickly seen by Jesus' followers as central to all they believed. Within a few weeks of Jesus' death, Peter was saying to the crowds in Jerusalem,

'In accordance with his own plan God had already decided that Jesus would be handed over to you; and you killed him by letting sinful men crucify him.'

So why is the cross so important to Christianity?

The cross in today's culture
The cross today is a symbol that has become commonplace in our culture. Crosses appear in graveyards, in public places, on flags, and even round people's necks, worn as jewellery. As a result, the symbol of the cross has been largely drained of its original meaning. It is worn and used by people who have no belief in, nor awareness of the death of Jesus. It is easy to forget what the cross actually represents.

The cross in Roman times
If a Roman citizen from the time of Jesus were alive today, he would be horrified to see people actually wearing a cross round their necks. The cross was a picture of public disgrace, torture and death. Crucifixion was something of which to be ashamed rather than proud, so the cross was not used as a decorated ornament. It would be rather like a person wearing a noose or an electric chair round their necks today.

Crucifixion was a Roman method of execution which they had borrowed from the Phoenicians. The Jewish practice was to stone condemned people to death. Crucifixion was the most humiliating and degrading way for a person to die, and the Romans used it in part to make an example of the person being crucified.

Was the death of Jesus a tragedy?
The cross meant torture, humiliation and death, so how can Christians view Jesus' death

as anything other than a tragedy? Jesus was a young man, he was innocent of the charges brought against him and his death was engineered by his enemies. Surely all these facts add up to a tragic event?

Jesus' death was no accident
The events of Jesus' crucifixion were terrible, but the cross was not simply the murder of an innocent man. It was not an accident. During his life, Jesus often spoke with his disciples about the future, and told them that they should expect him to be killed in this way. He said,

We are going up to Jerusalem, and everything that is written by the prophets about the Son of man will be fulfilled. He will be handed over to the Gentiles. They will mock him, insult him, spit on him, flog him and kill him. Luke 18: 31, 32

Jesus saw his approaching death as part of the work God had given him to do: the most important part of that work. Likening his coming death to an ordeal, he once said,

I have a baptism to undergo, and how distressed I am until it is completed! Luke 12: 50

Mark's Gospel gives us a vivid glimpse of Jesus striding ahead of his disciples in his eagerness to

THE CRUCIFIXION

Luke's account of Jesus' execution:

When they came to the placed called The Skull, there they crucified him, along with the criminals — one on his right, the other on his left. Jesus said 'Father, forgive them, for they do not know what they are doing.' And they divided up his clothing by casting lots. The people stood watching, and the rulers even sneered at him. They said 'He saved others; let him save himself if he is the Christ of God, the Chosen One.' The soldiers also came up and mocked him. They offered him wine vinegar and said, 'If you are the king of the Jews, save yourself.' There was a written notice above him, which read: 'This is the king of the Jews.'

One of the criminals who hung there hurled insults at him: 'Aren't you the Christ? Save yourself and us!' But the other criminal rebuked him, 'Don't you fear God,' he said, 'since you are under the same sentence? We are punished justly, for we are getting what our deeds deserve. But this man has done nothing wrong.' Then he said, 'Jesus, remember me when you come into your kingdom.' Jesus answered him, 'I tell you the truth, today you will be with me in paradise.'

It was now about the sixth hour, and darkness came over the whole land until the ninth hour, for the sun stopped shining. And the curtain of the temple was torn in two. Jesus called out with a loud voice, 'Father, into your hands I commit my spirit.' When he had said this, he breathed his last. The centurion, seeing what had happened, praised God and said, 'Surely this was a righteous man.' When all the people who had gathered to witness this sight saw what took place, they beat their breasts and went away. But all those who knew him, including the women who had followed him from Galilee, stood at a distance, watching these things. *Luke 23 : 33-49*

reach Jerusalem and the final act of his life:

Jesus and his disciples were now on the road going up to Jerusalem. Jesus was going ahead of the disciples, who were filled with alarm; the people who followed behind were afraid.
Mark 10: 32

Clearly Jesus' arrest and death were no surprise to him.

The greater tragedy
Jesus told his disciples that he had come on a rescue mission –

When people wear crosses, it is sometimes just for decoration. But the cross is really a powerful symbol of forgiveness and new life.

to rescue men and women from the dilemma of sin. The cross was at the heart of this rescue mission. So while the cross was something of a tragedy, it only happened because people had gone wrong in the first place.

The tragedy is bigger than the events of that first Good Friday in Jerusalem. It started when people first turned their backs on God and decided to live to please themselves. And it continues whenever we live selfishly, mistreating other people or abusing the gifts God has given us. That is the greater tragedy: our own sinfulness.

The symbol of mankind's sin
Jesus was humiliated on the cross. But in a real sense, all those who took part in bringing about his death were humiliated too. The suffering and death of Jesus make very uncomfortable reading. In that story, we see things that we would prefer to

❝God demonstrates his own love for us in this: While we were still sinners, Christ died for us. ❞

ignore. We see the murderous spite of the Sanhedrin and the weakness of Pilate; we see the anger of the mob and the brutality of the soldiers. It is hardly a moment in history to be proud of.

The cross shows up humanity in the worst possible light. We cannot attach blame to those who took part without recognizing some of their weaknesses and motives in ourselves. The cross shows us our desperate condition.

The symbol of God's love

The cross shows us more than the truth about ourselves; it also shows us the truth about God's love. The death of Jesus gives us a picture of the enormous love God has for us, even though we are in rebellion against him. He was prepared to go as far as to send his own Son to die, to free us from sin and death.

The cross therefore gives us a symbol both of our need of God's help and of his amazing response to that need. That is why the cross is absolutely central to the whole of the Christian message. It is good news about what God has done.

What is sin?

Can we still talk about 'sin' in the twentieth century? Surely 'sin' is an old fashioned and negative word that implies fixed standards of right and wrong. Who can say what is right and what is not today?

Right and wrong

Many people today believe that there are no solid rules of right and wrong behaviour, such as the Ten Commandments in the Old Testament. We all have to be true to ourselves, so it is said, and decide what is good for us, and what will do us harm. Yet, in practice every society decides that certain types of behaviour *are* wrong, and punishes those who do what is unacceptable. The laws of any land constitute fixed, solid standards of right and wrong.

Christians believe that we can know what is right and what is wrong in at least two ways.

Firstly, God has made us so that we can distinguish between right and wrong, giving us a conscience which sets off an alarm signal whenever we cross over the line into evil. Secondly, God has told us in the Bible the kind of behaviour that pleases him. This does not mean that everything is black and white. There are areas where we cannot be absolutely sure of the right course of action. But all the same, many of our decisions are still a simple choice between right and wrong.

We are responsible

We may like to call sin by other names. We can talk about

making mistakes. Or we may try to understand why people go wrong by looking at their social background, the way their parents brought them up or faults in their personality. All this is valid and extremely helpful in understanding people; it may lead to more healthy living conditions. By recognizing social problems today, we understand more fully that sin works in society, and not merely in individuals.

But to say that sin is a social problem does not clear us as individuals from responsibility for our own actions. Sin is also an individual problem. Our background, environment and upbringing will all affect the way that we develop as people, but they do not completely explain why we do wrong or mean that we cannot responsibly choose

These men, who were rescued from a labour camp where they were forced to work as loggers without pay, remind us that slavery has existed throughout history. The New Testament uses the picture of redemption from slavery to describe our release through Jesus' death from the power of evil.

between right and wrong. Christians believe that God has made us responsible for ourselves, and that he is pleased when we act responsibly towards each other.

Sin in action
The Bible pictures sin in a large number of ways. Sin is like failing to hit a target, or failing to reach an expected standard. To sin means to wander away from the right road, to get lost in the

66 **All have sinned and fall short of the glory of God. 99**

darkness or to fall into a hole. To sin is to be caught fast in a trap.

At its worst, sin is not a mistake – quite the reverse. We may know what the right course of action is, but sin by not taking it, or even by deliberately taking the wrong course. Paul the apostle goes even further when he describes people as slaves to the power of sin:

Even though the desire to do good is in me, I am not able to do it. I don't do the good I want to do; instead, I do the evil that I do not want to do.
Romans 7: 18, 19

Sin is more than doing wrong
Sin, then, is more than something that we do. It is not so much *doing* wrong, as *being* wrong. If you look at the leaves of a tree, you can tell what kind of tree it is. In the same way, we can tell

what kind of person we are faced with. We act sinfully because we are sinful. The Bible says that sin has gone right down to the roots of our being, and this is why we are always inclined to do what is wrong.

The problem of sin

We cannot control sin in our lives. When we try to do so, we find out just how powerful a grip it has on us. This problem of personal sin is also mirrored in the problems of our world. Despite conferences, arms talks, diplomacy and genuine attempts by governments, we still have starvation, brutal dictatorships, the irresponsibility of pollution, and the arms trade. At the root of all these problems is the problem of sin; it is our greatest dilemma.

Jesus did not mince words when he talked about the human situation. He spoke of the source of the world's evil:

It is what comes out of a person that makes him unclean. For from the inside, from a person's heart, come the evil ideas which lead him to do immoral things, to rob, kill, commit adultery, be greedy, and do all sorts of evil things; deceit, indecency, jealousy, slander, pride, and folly – all these evil things come from inside a person and make him unclean. Mark 7: 20 – 23

Our sinfulness requires a solution.

How is Jesus' death a solution to sin?

If sin is the root of all the problems that afflict humanity, how can the death of one man, a carpenter who became a teacher all those years ago in a small, far-away country, be a solution to the sins of all people? To answer this question we need to look at an event in the history of the people of Israel.

Slavery

Each year, the Jewish people still celebrate what is known as 'the Passover'. They eat a simple meal together as a family and remember the time when their ancestors were enslaved in the land of Egypt. For years the Israelites were forced by the Egyptians to do hard labour and were cruelly oppressed. Eventually a law was passed which demanded that all newborn male Israelites were to be drowned, to prevent their race from growing in numbers.

The Passover meal, celebrating Israel's deliverance from Egypt in Moses' day, is still a high point of the Jewish year. The last supper which Jesus ate with his disciples was at Passover time. Jesus took the Passover symbols of bread and wine and applied them to deliverance from sin through his death.

In the middle of all this, God called a young Hebrew to lead his people to freedom. His name was Moses. Freeing the Israelites proved to be a very difficult task, as the Egyptian Pharaoh was determined to stop God's people leaving Egypt. Despite a series of plagues sent from God, Pharaoh remained firm and refused the Israelites their freedom.

The Passover

So God finally gave Moses instructions for the first Passover. He told Moses that he was going to kill all the firstborn sons in Egypt, but he would spare the Israelites if they obeyed his instructions. Each Hebrew family was to kill a lamb, roast it and eat it together at night. With the lamb they were to eat bitter herbs, and they were to eat the meal quickly with their sandals and cloaks on and with a staff in their hands to show they were prepared to leave Egypt soon.

They were to take some of the lamb's blood and paint it over the top and sides of the doorframe of their houses, on the outside. This would be a sign that those who lived inside were obedient to God. When God saw the blood he would 'pass over' the house and not harm the eldest son of the house.

It all happened as God had said. At midnight, the firstborn sons of Egypt were struck dead – from the son of Pharaoh to the son of the poorest prisoner in Pharaoh's dungeon. But those homes which had the blood painted over their doors were passed over by God. That same night, Pharaoh sent for Moses and told him to get out of Egypt and take the Israelites with him.

Because God delivered his people from oppression in this way, the Israelites were told to celebrate the Passover meal for ever. By eating the meal together as a family, they would remember the time when they were slaves in Egypt, and give thanks to God for the night he delivered them.

Jesus and the Passover

In the time of Jesus, the Passover was celebrated in Jerusalem every year. Jesus died during the week when pilgrims were pouring into the city to celebrate the Passover. Because the Passover lamb was at the very centre of the celebrations, the first Christians used the image of the lamb as a natural way of talking about the meaning of Jesus' death.

Paul wrote to Corinth:

REMEMBERING JESUS' DEATH

All Jews celebrate the Passover to remember the time when God delivered his people from the Egyptians. Christians all over the world remember the death of Jesus, and celebrate the time when God freed his people from sin. Jesus specifically commanded his first disciples to make this remembrance as he took a last supper with them on the night he was arrested:

The day came during the Festival of Unleavened Bread when the lambs for the Passover meal were to be killed . Jesus sent off Peter and John with these instructions: 'Go and get the Passover meal ready for us to eat.'

When the hour came, Jesus took his place at the table with the apostles. He said to them, 'I have wanted so much to eat this Passover meal with you before I suffer! For I tell you, I will never eat it until It Is given its full meaning in the kingdom of God.'

Then Jesus took a cup, gave thanks to God, and said, 'Take this and share it among yourselves. I tell you that from now on I will not drink this wine until the kingdom of God comes.'

Then he took a piece of bread, gave thanks to God, broke it, and gave it to them, saying 'This is my body, which is given for you. Do this in memory of me.' In the same way, he gave them the cup after the supper, saying, 'This cup is God's new covenant sealed with my blood, which is poured out for you.' *Luke 22 : 7, 8, 14-20*

**For Christ, our Passover lamb,
has been sacrificed. Therefore let
us keep the Festival . . .**
1 Corinthians 5: 7

Paul's readers would understand
that he was using the language of
the Passover to say that Jesus
Christ had set them free. As the
Israelites had been set free from
slavery at the time of the exodus,
so now the sacrifice of Jesus set
people free from the power of sin.

Sacrifice
Many Western people have
difficulties with the idea of
sacrifice, seeing it as a barbaric
practice. Sacrifice certainly is
horrific – but so, in God's eyes, is
our sin. Sacrifice was intended as
a way to remove the problem of
sin. So the extreme and
distasteful nature of sacrifice
only mirrored the extreme and
distasteful nature of sin.
Desperate diseases require
desperate remedies.

So, in the time of the Old
Testament, the problem of sin
was dealt with through a system
of animal sacrifices. For the
person who took part in a
sacrifice, the significance lay in
what the sacrifice represented.
The person would bring an
animal to be sacrificed and
would lay his hands on the head
of the animal to show God that he
wished to be identified with it.
Then, by killing it, he declared
that because of his sins he
himself deserved to die, but that
the animal was dying in his
place. These sacrifices had to be
made again and again. They
were not a perfect solution to the
problem of sin.

Jesus' death as a sacrifice
The New Testament sees the
death of Jesus as the perfect
sacrifice, which only needed to
be made once and for all. His
death was perfect because he
had lived a completely sinless
life, and therefore did not deserve any punishment for sin. So,
when Jesus died, God could accept
his death for the sins of others,
setting people free from the
penalty and power of sin.

John the Baptist once pointed
his disciples towards Jesus,

**Look, the Lamb of God, who
takes away the sin of the world!**
John 1: 29

In the Old Testament, lambs had
to be offered continually because
they were not an effective
solution to sin. But, because the
death of Jesus was a perfect
solution, it only needed to happen
once. Whenever we go to God to
ask him to forgive our sins –
which we do often throughout our
lives – we can ask confidently,
because of that one sacrifice
Jesus made.

There are other pictures in the
New Testament that tell us what
the death of Jesus meant, but the
sacrifice picture is the central
one. The other pictures speak
more about what resulted from
Jesus' death, but the picture of
sacrifice shows us *how* his death
takes away our sin.

What did Jesus' death achieve?

Just as the Bible gives us many different pictures of what sin is, and what sin has done, so there are different pictures of what Jesus' death has achieved for us.

Victory

The death of Jesus is seen in the New Testament as a battle against the person who has power in the world – the devil. Jesus himself saw his approaching death in these

Jesus died to bring people back into relationship with God and with each other. Everything that stood between people and God he took upon himself on the cross.

terms. During the last week of his life, he said,

Now is the time for this world to be judged; now the ruler of this world will be overthrown.
John 12: 31

On the cross he won a great victory over mankind's greatest enemy.

Bought back

The New Testament borrows the imagery of the slave market to describe the effect on us of sin. Through our sins, we have become slaves to the power of evil, living in the fear of death.

The price that had to be paid to redeem us, or buy us back, from slavery was very high: the life of Jesus. He paid the necessary price, bringing us into a new freedom from sin. Jesus once said,

The Son of man did not come to be served, but to serve, and to give his life as a ransom for many. Mark 10: 45

Paul the apostle adds,

The reason why Jesus Christ lived and died was to rescue humanity. Because we have failed to live as God intended, we cannot save ourselves.

Freedom is what we have – Christ has set us free! Stand, then, as free people, and do not allow yourselves to become slaves again. Galatians 5: 1

This does not mean that we are completely free of the problem of sin; Christians are by no means perfect in their behaviour! But we are under new management. We once lived under the rule of sin. Now we are owned by God, who has bought us with the death of his Son. He gives us his power to begin to live life under his rule.

Justified

Paul the apostle uses the language of the law-courts to describe how we stand before God and what Jesus' death has achieved. Paul is concerned to show that God does not forgive our sins by shutting his eyes and pretending that they were never there. God, he says, is a God of justice, who has shown mankind the way in which he should live. If people refuse to live that way, God will have to punish them. Paul's picture of God is not of a sadistic ogre who longs to punish people, but of a good judge who has no alternative but to implement the law.

Paul puts humanity in the dock and shows that we are guilty of not keeping God's laws. God longs to forgive us, but being a God of justice he cannot simply forget our sin. The solution to this problem of justice lay in the death of Jesus. Paul says,

In the death of Jesus, God mounted a rescue operation on a grand scale. No lesser solution would have been adequate to the disaster of a world spoiled and distorted by human sinfulness.

God offered him, so that by his death he should become the means by which people's sins are forgiven through their faith in him. Romans 3: 25

The person who has faith in Jesus Christ is forgiven by God, because God accepts the punishment that Jesus received on the cross as a substitute for that person's punishment.

In this way, God the judge can declare the guilty person cleared of guilt, and through Jesus God shows his love for all people. Those who believe in Jesus Christ have been acquitted and set free.

Reconciled

In an age where the divorce rate is high and getting higher, the picture of Jesus' death as a means of reconciliation is a powerful one. Many passages in the Bible talk about the effect of sin in cutting us off from the friendship of God. One Old Testament prophet, Hosea, said that God's relationship with his people is like a marriage which has ended in divorce, because the people have been unfaithful in following other gods.

From our own experience, we know that whenever a relationship has been broken, somebody has to make the first move to bring about a healing of the pain and bitterness. Making the first move is always a difficult and costly business. The New Testament sees Jesus as the one who did this. He came as a peacemaker, seeking to bring about a restoration of good relationships between people and God.

Jesus brought about this peace by dying on the cross. Paul expresses it in this way:

At one time you were far away from God and were his enemies because of the evil things you did and thought. But now, by means of the physical death of his Son, God has made you his friends, in order to bring you, holy, pure, and faultless, into his presence.
Colossians 1: 21, 22

Jesus' death has reconciled us to God, and we know again the joy of his company.

Salvation

All these pictures show us that God has acted to save us. Each of them expresses God's salvation in a different way. We were slaves, but now we are free. We

66 Christ died for sins once for all . . . to bring you to God. 99

have been found guilty and worthy of death, but now we are acquitted. We were God's enemies, but now we have been made his friends. The death of Jesus has reversed the condition we were in, and has brought us back to the place God has always meant us to be – with himself.

This is why, almost, 2,000 years later, Christians still see the crucifixion of Jesus as the most important single event in history, and an awareness of its meaning as the most vital awareness in their own experience. It is only because Jesus was prepared to suffer that we have received the love and forgiveness of God.

10
RESURRECTION

Is the resurrection important?

For Christians who celebrate Easter, the high point of the week is Easter Sunday morning, when they remember the resurrection of Jesus Christ from the dead. It is an ancient church tradition for the minister to say, 'The Lord is risen!', to which the congregation respond, 'He is risen indeed!'

Christians today see Jesus' resurrection as a key element in their faith. But how did the early Christians understand the resurrection?

Frightened disciples

For the disciples everything had gone horribly wrong. Their plans for Jesus to be the new ruler of Israel had received a boost when he had entered Jerusalem to the cheers and support of a crowd. But in a few hurried hours he had been arrested, tried, condemned and executed. Suddenly, the person who had commanded all their attention and loyalty over the last three years had gone for ever. And they were terrified that the authorities would now track them down and do the same to them.

Then came that remarkable Sunday that was to change them completely. Once they had met the risen Jesus, they began to understand for the first time the true nature of his mission. For them, this experience was the beginning of a new life.

The preaching of the early church

From the very beginning of the church's life, the resurrection had a vital place in the message the apostles preached. The book of Acts records many sermons preached by the early church. In each of them the resurrection is more than merely something to believe in. It is the key factor that changed Jesus' seeming defeat on the cross into a great victory over death.

On the first day of the church's life, Peter spoke to a crowd in Jerusalem:

In accordance with his own plan God had already decided that Jesus would be handed over to you; and you killed him by letting sinful men crucify him. But God raised him from death, setting him free from its power,

because it was impossible that
death should hold him prisoner.'
Acts 2: 23, 24

Paul's view of the resurrection
The apostle Paul went even
further. In a letter to the
Christians in Corinth, who were
having doubts about the reality of
Jesus' resurrection, he said that
the resurrection gave meaning to
the Christian faith. Without it,
there would be absolutely no
point in being a Christian:

'If Christ has not been raised
from death, then we have nothing
to preach and you have nothing
to believe.' 1 Corinthians 15: 14

The resurrection of Jesus gave
meaning to his whole life and to
his death.

Essential belief
If the Christian faith is like a
building, then the resurrection is
a vital part of the foundations.
The confident claim that Jesus
did not remain dead in his grave
is a major New Testament
theme. Because of its crucial
importance, we need to be
absolutely sure that it is
reasonable to believe in it. The
Christian faith stands or falls on
the question of the resurrection
of Jesus.

Did Jesus really
rise from death?

A great deal of evidence can be presented in support of
Jesus' resurrection. But if we begin by believing that it is
impossible for someone to rise from death, then we will be
able to think of alternative ways to explain this evidence.
Only if we are open to the possibility that supernatural
events can occur, will we be able to consider the evidence
with a more open mind.

In examining the evidence that the New Testament
makes available to us, we have to judge whether or not
the resurrection is a *reasonable explanation* of what
took place. The Gospels cannot give us *concrete proof* of
the resurrection, but we can ask whether they give us
good reason to believe in it.

From the day the resurrection was reported to have
happened until today, people have objected to it for a wide
variety of reasons. In trying to examine the likelihood of
the event, it is important to meet these objections head-on

Someone else was crucified
This is an old interpretation of the events of the first Good Friday, and it appears in the Qur'an. According to this objection, in the turmoil before the crucifixion someone else was confused with the condemned prisoner, and was crucified instead of Jesus. The most likely candidate in this case of mistaken identity has been Simon of Cyrene. Luke tells us:

The soldiers led Jesus away, and as they were going, they met a man from Cyrene named Simon who was coming into the city from the country. They seized him, put the cross on him, and

THE FIRST DAY

John's account of Jesus' resurrection:

Early on the first day of the week, while it was still dark, Mary of Magdala went to the tomb and saw that the stone had been removed from the entrance. So she came running to Simon Peter and the other disciple, the one Jesus loved, and said, 'They have taken the Lord out of the tomb, and we don't know where they have put him!'

So Peter and the other disciple started for the tomb. Both were running, but the other disciple outran Peter and reached the tomb first. He bent over and looked in at the strips of linen lying there but did not go in. Then Simon Peter, who was behind him, arrived and went into the tomb. He saw the strips of linen lying there, as well as the burial cloth that had been around Jesus' head. The cloth was folded up by itself, separate from the linen. Finally the other disciple, who had reached the tomb first, also went inside. He saw and believed .

On the evening of that first day of the week, when the disciples were together, with the doors locked for fear of the Jews, Jesus came and stood among them and said, 'Peace be with you!' After he said this, he showed them his hands and his side. The disciples were overjoyed when they saw the Lord.

Again Jesus said, 'Peace be with you! As the Father has sent me, I am sending you.' And with that he breathed on them and said, 'Receive the Holy Spirit. If you forgive anyone his sins, they are forgiven; if you do not forgive them, they are not forgiven.'

Now Thomas (called Didymus), one of the Twelve, was not with the disciples when Jesus came. When the other disciples told him that they had seen the Lord, he declared, 'Unless I see the nail marks in his hands and put my finger where the nails were, and put my hand into his side, I will not believe it.'

A week later his disciples

were in the house again, and Thomas with them. Though the doors were locked, Jesus came and stood among them and said, 'Peace be with you!' Then he said to Thomas, 'put your finger here; see my hands. Reach out your hand and put it into my side. Stop doubting and believe.' Thomas answered, 'My Lord and my God!' Then Jesus told him, 'Because you have seen me, you have believed; blessed are those who have not seen and yet have believed.'

made him carry it behind Jesus.
Luke 23: 26

However, it is difficult to imagine that the Roman soldiers would so easily mistake a man walking into the city for the man they had been given to crucify, who had been flogged and beaten since the early hours of the morning. John's Gospel also tells us that several of Jesus' followers, including his mother, were close enough to the cross for Jesus to speak with them. They would hardly be likely to mistake another person for Jesus.

Jesus did not really die
A more recent theory claims that Jesus fainted on the cross and

It is never easy to cope with the death of someone close, but belief in life beyond the grave takes away any sense of hopelessness.

was mistakenly proclaimed dead. But after he had been buried, he revived in the coolness of the tomb, escaped and presented himself to the disciples as risen from the grave. This theory takes note of the report in the Gospels that Jesus seemed to die quickly. Such a quick death could indicate that Jesus had not died at all.

The theory raises more problems than it solves. Jesus did die quickly – but this attracted attention rather than diverting it. Instead of assuming that death had occurred, people began to question if it had actually happened so soon. Mark tells us:

Pilate was surprised to hear that Jesus was already dead. He called the army officer and asked him if Jesus had been dead a long time. After hearing the officer's report, Pilate told Joseph he could have the body. Mark 15: 44, 45

John's account adds a further detail. To hasten death, soldiers would often break the legs of crucified criminals to prevent them from breathing by pressing downwards. Hanging solely by their arms, they would suffocate. But when, after doing it to the other two men, they came to do this to Jesus, they found that he was already dead. John tells us that one of the soldiers made sure of this:

One of the soldiers, however, plunged his spear into Jesus' side, and at once blood and water poured out. John 19: 34

Quite apart from these circumstantial details, this alternative sounds like a tall order. Could Jesus, who had been flogged and hung on a cross for hours, have rolled back the heavy stone, overcome the Roman guard, and limped back to his followers, pretending to be the glorious victor over death?

The disciples visited the wrong tomb
Another explanation of the evidence presented in the Gospels is to say that the empty tomb found by the disciples was not that of Jesus. There must have been a large number of tombs around Jerusalem such as the one Jesus was placed in, so a mistake like this would have been possible.

Such a theory accounts for the discovery of the empty tomb, but it fails to explain the disappearance of Jesus' body. If the disciples began to preach about

> **66 Christ died for our sins . . . was buried . . . was raised on the third day. 99**

the resurrection of Jesus on the strength of the fact that his tomb was empty, then all the authorities needed to have done was to visit the correct tomb and produce his body. They certainly knew which tomb was the right one, yet they failed to produce the body to destroy the rumour of the resurrection.

The disciples stole Jesus' body
According to the early Christians, this theory was the invention of the chief priests and elders, which makes it the oldest objection to the resurrection. Matthew tells us that the soldiers who had guarded the tomb went to see the Jewish authorities:

The chief priests met with the elders and made their plan; they

WE ARE WITNESSES

Only a few weeks after the crucifixion, Peter said: 'You killed the one who leads to life, but God raised him from death — and we are witnesses to this.' The resurrection depends a lot for its credibility on early Christian witnesses, those who said they actually saw Jesus alive after death. The New Testament passages which report meetings with the risen Jesus are listed here:

Mary Magdalene	Matthew 28:1-10 Mark 16:1-8 Luke 24:1-11 John 20:11-18	(with 'the other Mary') (with Mary the mother of James, and Salome) (with Joanna, Mary the mother of James, and 'the other women')
Simon Peter	Luke 24:34 1 Corinthians 15:5	
The disciples	Matthew 28:16-20 Luke 24:36-49 John 20:19-23 John 20:24-29 John 21:1-24 Acts 1:6-11 1 Corinthians 15:5 1 Corinthians 15:7	 (without Thomas) (with Thomas) (seven of the disciples, including Peter, James, John, Thomas and Nathanael) (especially Peter) (with James, the brother of Jesus)
Cleopas and another follower of Jesus	Luke 24:13-32	
500 followers	1 Corinthians 15:6	('Then he appeared to more than 500 of his followers at once, most of whom are still alive, although some have died.')
Paul	Acts 9:1-6 1 Corinthians 15:8	

gave a large sum of money to the soldiers and said, 'You are to say that his disciples came during the night and stole his body while you were asleep.' Matthew 28: 12, 13

Whether or not Matthew's accusation is true, the story was certainly a good one. The disciples would surely have the motive for stealing Jesus' body, they could then say that he was alive, as he had promised them. The authorities would be able to do little to stop the rumour as they would have no body with which to support their argument.

But the question is, why would the disciples steal the body? John's Gospel records in a few words a tiny but important detail:

They still did not understand the scripture which said that he must rise from death. John 20: 9

Despite Jesus' predictions about his suffering, death and resurrection, the disciples had not remembered his words. Possibly they had been so confused by the unexpected prediction of his death that the prediction of his resurrection was not even heard.

In any case, the disciples were beaten, disillusioned men. They hid behind locked doors fearing the same fate as their teacher. And when we are told that Jesus did appear to them, they were

The resurrection declares God's principle of life in death.

slow to believe what they saw. But more important, having invented this story, would they have been prepared to die for believing in it? Many of the disciples died for their faith in the risen Jesus, and none of them ever admitted that the resurrection was false.

The authorities removed the body

Another possible explanation of the evidence is that the Jewish authorities removed Jesus' body to prevent the disciples from raiding the tomb. Matthew tells us that there was some anxiety about this among the Jewish leaders, and although the disciples had forgotten about the prediction of Jesus' resurrection, the authorities certainly had not.

The next day, which was a Sabbath, the chief priests and the Pharisees met with Pilate and said, 'Sir, we remember that while that liar was still alive he said, "I will be raised to life three days later." Give orders, then, for his tomb to be carefully guarded until the third day, so that his disciples will not be able to go and steal the body, and then tell the people that he was raised from death.' Matthew 27: 62 – 64

Setting such a guard seems to make the removal of the body unnecessary. However, the fatal weakness of this argument is the dismal failure of the authorities to produce the body of Jesus in answer to the disciples' claim that he had risen from death. This would have been the ultimate proof that the resurrection was a lie.

The accounts do not agree
Many critics of the resurrection have pointed to the fact that there are contradictions in the four accounts, and have said that the evidence they present is therefore unreliable. The differences in the accounts range from small details such as the number of angels, to more difficult problems. Why would the women come to anoint the body of Jesus on Sunday morning, according to Luke, when John tells us that Nicodemus and Joseph had already done this on Friday night? And why does Luke record that the two disciples who met the risen Jesus outside Jerusalem returned to be greeted with joy by the other disciples, when Mark records that they were greeted with unbelief?

Although we may say that the four writers were approaching

> **66** God has raised this very Jesus from death, and we are all witnesses to this fact. **99**

the resurrection from different angles, and therefore would have differences of emphasis, we cannot deny that there are discrepancies. Yet in one sense

this may be a strength. Any dramatic incident (such as a car accident) will be told quite differently by different witnesses. It seems that the four Gospel writers drew on a wide range of eye-witnesses who had not collaborated with each other in getting the details of the story right. None of them had expected the resurrection, and each of them remembered what had struck him or her most vividly.

'The real Easter miracle'
Some people who have discounted the possibility that Jesus actually rose from the grave have said that the real Easter miracle lay in the disciples being transformed and coming to believe in the risen Jesus. Certainly, the change that took place in the disciples was remarkable. But what could have brought about such an astonishing transformation? The Gospel accounts give us reasonable cause for the change in the disciples – a powerful series of meetings with the risen Jesus. If Jesus did not rise, then how else would the disciples have been changed?

Hallucinations
One common explanation offered is that the disciples had a vision or hallucinated when they 'saw' Jesus alive again. In the intensity of their anguish over the death of their leader, they had a religious experience which convinced them that Jesus was still alive.

But this objection fails to

Jesus appeared to his disciples a number of times after his death. Once he cooked and ate a fish breakfast with them beside the Sea of Galilee. This was no ghost or hallucination but a unique new level of life.

account for the facts in a number of ways. It does not explain the mystery of the empty tomb. Why was the body missing? Also, the record of the resurrection appearances tells us about a remarkably physical Jesus – remarkable, that is, for a hallucination. Jesus ate fish, broke bread, allowed a sceptical disciple to feel his wounds and cooked them all breakfast.

Nor do the Gospel accounts allow us to dismiss these appearances as a kind of mass hysteria. Jesus appeared to individuals as well as to the disciples as a whole, and there were independent reports of the same experience. The two disciples who met with Jesus on the road to Emmaus raced back to tell the others in Jerusalem, only to find that they had met with him.

Women and others
If the resurrection stories were invented, then their authors included some very strange, even damaging details, that put a poor light on the disciples' behaviour. First, there is the role of the women. In the time of Jesus, women were non-people. They sat apart from the men in

the synagogues, were not allowed to give evidence in court and were regarded as the carriers of idle gossip.

But of all the characters in the resurrection stories, it is the women who showed the greatest willingness to believe. The only person who appears in all four of the Gospel resurrection accounts is Mary Magdalene. And the women were given the important task of telling the apostles the good news. In the male-oriented world of the time, no author would include this detail unless it actually happened.

People who come to believe that Jesus was raised from death find a new purpose and a new joy in their lives.

In contrast, the men come off badly. While the women are outside, going to prepare spices

66 **Mary of Magdala went to the disciples with the news: 'I have seen the Lord!'** 99

to anoint the body of Jesus, the men are inside, locked in and fearful for their own lives. And how did these men first react when they were told about the event that was to become one of the most important truths of Christianity?

Many lawyers have considered the evidence for believing that Jesus rose again, and have concluded that this evidence is stronger than most that is used in courts of law. The nature of the eye-witness reports, including their slight contradictions on points of detail, is exactly as an experienced lawyer would expect to find it.

The apostles thought that what the women said was nonsense, and they did not believe them.
Luke 24: 11

Such details would be very curious if they had been invented by the Christians.

Do the stories ring true?
The Gospel writers did not set out to provide their readers with *proof* that Jesus was alive. They wrote to recount the details of what happened, so that their readers should have good reasons to believe in the res-urrection. Christians believe that the evidence we have for the resurrection of Jesus would be strong enough to stand up in a court of law.

If we think, after examining the evidence, that the stories do ring true, then we need to ask whether we are willing to believe that Jesus actually rose from the dead. To accept that belief is not like accepting any other historical fact. It has implic-ations for the way we live our lives. We may have to start looking at Jesus in a new way.

What does the resurrection mean?

The early church believed that the resurrection was indispensable to their Christian faith. But why was it so important to them? If Jesus made it possible for us to have our sins forgiven by dying on the cross, what more did he need to do? What was the point of the resurrection?

Jesus is alive

The resurrection takes the Christian faith out of the realm of theory and into everyday living. Without the resurrection, the teaching of Jesus would simply be an interesting collection of stories, or a system of rules that we would find impossibly hard to keep. But because Jesus is alive, he challenges us to follow him, and gives us the power to start living out his teaching ourselves.

The New Testament outside the Gospels talks about Jesus not as a dead and remembered teacher, but as a living person who still works through those who follow him. Paul writes:

Since you have accepted Christ Jesus as Lord, live in union with him. Keep your roots deep in him, build your lives on him, and become stronger in your faith, as you were taught.
Colossians 2: 6, 7

To be a Christian is not just to believe in certain things – it is to know and love Jesus Christ.

A stamp of approval

There is an important phrase in the New Testament which the first Christians used again and again in describing the resurrection: 'God raised him'. For example, in one of Peter's sermons in the book of Acts:

Then they put him to death by nailing him to a cross. But God raised him from death three days later . . .
Acts 10 : 39, 40

God the Father brought Jesus back to life to vindicate all that he had said and done. If Jesus had stayed dead, his prediction that he would be killed and then rise from the dead would have been only half-true. More important, if the resurrection had not happened, Jesus' claims to forgive sin, to be the resurrection and the life, even to be the Son of God, would all have been a pack of lies. So by raising him from death, God publicly demonstrated the truth of Jesus' life.

N

THE HOPE OF THE RESURRECTION

Godfrey Williams, a university lecturer dying of Hodgkins' Disease, had something to say in an earlier chapter on miracles. Here he tells us what difference a belief in Jesus' resurrection makes when you are facing death:

The reason I am having to think about death at the rather tender age of thirty is that the medical profession think that I probably have no more than a few months to live. Now most people are either thinking about that after the age of about sixty or seventy, or they are not thinking about it at all because they die quickly. So I have had time to think, and in a way to prepare, and I think that has been quite a privilege. You realize that you are not ready to meet your Maker, and that there are things that should be put right in your life. And I have been happy with that privilege.

The resurrection of Jesus Christ is absolutely crucial to a Christian's hope in a life beyond this one. First of all, the resurrection is the ground of our faith. If the resurrection of Christ has not happened, then, as Paul said, we of all men are to be pitied, because we have no assurance that God loves us. We have no assurance that what Jesus said when he was on earth should be treated with any more respect than any other person who opens his mouth when he is on the earth. The resurrection is also crucial because it shows us that there is something after this life. If you like, Jesus has said, 'Look, I am raised from the dead, and you too will be raised from the dead.' That gives us our hope in a future after death — that we will be raised with some sort of similar structure to our own identities that we have now, and that we will be able to join God and enjoy living with him in the future.

The defeat of death

Jesus' resurrection was not an isolated incident in history. The New Testament tells us that Jesus will share with us his victory over death, by raising us too from death. So the resurrection of Jesus is only the first of many resurrections. Paul the apostle expresses it this way:

But the truth is that Christ has been raised from death, as the guarantee that those who sleep in death will also be raised.
1 Corinthians 15: 20

If we are certain that Jesus was raised from death, we can also be certain that he will give us life after our own death.

Jesus himself spoke before his death about sharing his resurrection with all people. He said,

I am the resurrection and the life. He who believes in me will live, even though he dies . . .
John 11: 25

And another time he spoke of our resurrection in the most graphic terms:

I am telling you the truth: the time is coming – the time has already come – when the dead will hear the voice of the Son of God, and those who hear it will come to life. John 5: 25

The resurrection and us

If it is true, as Christians claim, that the resurrection actually happened, we have to start thinking about Jesus differently. We can no longer think of him merely as Jesus the imaginative storyteller, or Jesus the profound moral teacher. If Jesus has defeated death, he must be Jesus the Lord, who can give us confidence in a life with him beyond death – and claim our loyalty and love in this life too. That is why it is vital to discover for ourselves whether the resurrection of Jesus took place or not. Our view of Jesus depends on it.

11

THE SPIRIT

Can we believe in the ascension?

Many people find it difficult to take the ascension seriously. Does the New Testament really expect us to believe that Jesus literally rose off the ground and went up through the clouds? And if so, what was the point of it all?

The ascension and the resurrection

Belief in the ascension really goes hand in hand with belief in the resurrection. Once we accept that Jesus physically rose from his grave, we then have to explain why he is no longer physically around.

The New Testament writers have no problem with this – they all assume that, although Jesus is no longer physically present, he is nonetheless still alive and reunited with his Father. They all assume that the resurrection appearances came to an end at some point, and there is no New Testament alternative to the ascension as the means by which that happened.

Is heaven 'up there'?

Many people see the ascension as a classic example of the belief that heaven is literally 'up there', that hell is below us, and so on. Modern science has shown that these ideas, prevalent in the time of the Bible, are now outdated. Therefore we should discard the idea of the ascension in the same way that we have discarded the idea that the sun goes around the earth or that the earth is flat.

Jesus exalted

But does the ascension really imply all those ideas? Far from going into strange details or theories about the ascension, the New Testament has a very simple point to make about the ascension of Jesus. John tells us that Jesus said,

I came from the Father and entered the world; now I am leaving the world and going back to the Father.
John 16: 28

In other words, Jesus was returning to God, having completed the work that he had been sent to do.

By rising from the earth in the sight of his disciples, Jesus may well have been involved in an acted parable. That is, he was not showing heaven to be so many miles above the earth, but rather he was going to a place where God is *exalted*. He rose physically because this was the best way the disciples could understand that he was returning to God.

Height and exaltation
Height has always carried the idea of superiority. In the past, a king sat on a raised throne, and even today we speak of 'the height of success', 'the highest office in the land' or say that someone has 'risen to great heights'. The point of the ascension was that Jesus was returning victorious to his Father after his defeat of death – and the ascension certainly gives a graphic demonstration of that.

The forty-day period
But why did Jesus not return to his Father immediately after his resurrection? The New Testament tells us that he kept appearing to his disciples for a considerable period of time – forty days. In the book of Acts, Luke tells us,

For forty days after his death he appeared to them many times in ways that proved beyond doubt that he was alive. They saw him, and he talked with them about the kingdom of God. Acts 1: 3

Luke seems to suggest that there were at least two reasons for the delay in Jesus' ascension. By appearing to them in different

THE LAST THEY SAW OF JESUS

At the beginning of the Acts of the Apostles comes the story of Jesus' 'ascension':

After his suffering, Jesus showed himself to the apostles and gave many convincing proofs that he was alive. He appeared to them over a period of forty days and spoke about the kingdom of God. On one occasion, while he was eating with them, he gave them this command: 'Do not leave Jerusalem, but wait for the gift my Father promised, which you have heard me speak about. For John baptised with water, but in a few days you will be baptised with the Holy Spirit.'

So when they met together, they asked him, 'Lord, are you at this time going to restore the kingdom to Israel?' He said to them: 'It is not for you to know the times or dates the Father has set by his own authority. But you will receive power when the Holy Spirit comes on you; and you will be my witnesses in Jerusalem, and in all Judea and Samaria, and to the ends of the earth.'

After he said this, he was taken up before their very eyes, and a cloud hid him from their sight. They were looking intently up into the sky as he was going, when suddenly two men dressed in white stood beside them. 'Men of Galilee,' they said, 'why do you stand here looking into the sky? This same Jesus, who has been taken from you into heaven, will come back in the same way you have seen him go into heaven.' *Acts 1: 3-11*

places over a long period of time, Jesus allowed the disciples to become completely convinced that he was alive. During this period he also gave them detailed teaching about the meaning of his death and resurrection, and about the part they were to play. The disciples had held on to many wrong ideas about Jesus during their time with him, but now Jesus was able to explain to them the things that had long puzzled them.

The promise of the Spirit
Finally, Jesus told them to wait for the Holy Spirit before beginning their work. According to Luke, the last words of Jesus before his ascension were,

But when the Holy Spirit comes upon you, you will be filled with power, and you will be witnesses for me in Jerusalem, in all Judea and Samaria, and to the ends of the earth.
Acts 1: 8

Who is the Holy Spirit?

On and after the Day of Pentecost, the Holy Spirit was very much the driving force behind the activity of the church. But who was the Spirit? Had he existed before this time?

A personality
The Spirit certainly existed before Pentecost, because the New Testament tells us that the Holy Spirit is God himself. The Holy Spirit had been active both in the life of Jesus and in Old Testament times.

In modern language, the word 'spirit' can often mean an impersonal force or an ideal. For example, people talk about having 'the spirit of courage' or of doing something 'in the right spirit'. The New Testament does not talk about the Holy Spirit in this impersonal way, as though he was merely a force. The early Christians saw the Spirit as fully and in every sense a *person*,

the one who guided the direction of the early church.

The Spirit in the Old Testament
In the Old Testament, God's Spirit was active in a limited way. His work was to give people God's power to do or say a particular thing which they could not do without God's help. For example, God told the prophet Jeremiah to tell the people of Israel that he would punish them by allowing foreign rulers to conquer them. To speak such a message was treason, and Jeremiah needed God's strength to have the courage to proclaim this message.

So the Spirit was given to those

who were called to do a special task for God. He worked only in a few individuals, and only for limited periods of time. Some of the Old Testament prophets longed for the time when God would give his Spirit to *all* God's people, and on a permanent basis. The prophet Ezekiel expressed this hope by saying:

I (God) will give you a new heart and a new mind. I will take away your stubborn heart of stone and give you an obedient heart. I will put my spirit in you and I will see to it that you follow my laws and keep all the commands I have given you. Ezekiel 36: 26, 27

So by giving his Spirit to people, God would not just be *telling* them to obey him, he would *help* them to do so.

Jesus and the Spirit
The four Gospel writers present Jesus as the person whose whole life was lived in the power of

'The wind blows wherever it wishes,' said Jesus. 'You hear the sound it makes, but you do not know where it comes from or where it is going. It is like that with everyone who is born of the Spirit.'

God's Spirit. Luke, for example, tells us that Jesus was conceived by the power of the Spirit. At his baptism, the Spirit appeared in the form of a dove, giving Jesus God's energy for all that lay ahead.

Jesus also said that he was able to start the work of God's kingdom because he had been given God's power:

The Spirit of the Lord is on me, because he has anointed me to preach good news to the poor.
Luke 4: 18

And another time, when Jesus' enemies said that he cast out demons by the power of Beelzebub (a Jewish name for the devil), he replied,

No, it is not Beelzebub, but God's Spirit, who gives me the power to drive out demons, which proves that the kingdom of God has already come upon you.
Matthew 12: 28

The disciples and the Spirit
Jesus told his disciples that soon they too would be able to receive the Spirit, and live in God's power. He said,

If you then, though you are evil, know how to give good gifts to your children, how much more will your Father in heaven give the Holy Spirit to those who ask him! Luke 11: 12, 13

However, it is in John's account of the Last Supper that we see Jesus' most explicit teaching about the coming of the Spirit. Jesus told the disciples that soon he would be leaving them, but that he and the Father would send them the Holy Spirit to be with them permanently – as the Old Testament prophets had hoped. The Spirit would use them to continue and extend the work that Jesus had begun.

Calling the Spirit 'the Helper', Jesus said these words:

I will ask the Father, and he will give you another Helper, who will stay with you for ever. He is the Spirit who reveals the truth about God. John 14: 16, 17

The Day of Pentecost
The disciples waited in Jerusalem after the ascension of Jesus, as he had told them to do. About ten days after the ascension was the Jewish feast of Pentecost. This celebrated the completion of the barley harvest, and was a time of joy and thanksgiving when Jerusalem

❝ The Helper, the Holy Spirit, whom the Father will send in my name, will teach you everything. ❞

would be full of pilgrims.

On the day of the feast, Jesus' followers were filled with the power of the Holy Spirit and were given the ability to proclaim the good news about Jesus in the

THE DAY OF PENTECOST

The story of the Holy Spirit being given to the first Christians:

When the Day of Pentecost came, they were all together in one place. Suddenly a sound like the blowing of a violent wind came from heaven and filled the whole house where they were sitting. They saw what seemed to be tongues of fire that separated and came to rest on each of them. All of them were filled with the Holy Spirit and began to speak in other tongues as the Spirit enabled them.

Now there were staying in Jerusalem God-fearing Jews from every nation under heaven. When they heard this sound, a crowd came together in bewilderment, because each one heard them speaking in his own language. Utterly amazed, they asked: 'Are not all these men who are speaking Galileans? Then how is it that each of us hears them in his own native language?' . . . Amazed and perplexed they asked one another, 'What does this mean?' Some, however, made fun of them and said, 'They have had too much wine.'

Then Peter stood up with the Eleven, raised his voice and addressed the crowd: 'Fellow Jews and all of you who are in Jerusalem, let me explain this to you; listen carefully to what I say. These men are not drunk, as you suppose. It's only nine in the morning! No, this is what was spoken by the prophet Joel: "In the last days, God says, I will pour out my Spirit on all people. Your sons and daughters will prophesy, your young men will see visions, your old men will dream dreams."

'. . .Men of Israel, listen to this: Jesus of Nazareth was a man accredited by God to you by miracles, wonders and signs, which God did among you through him, as you yourselves know. This man was handed over to you by God's set purpose and foreknowledge; and you, with the help of wicked men, put him to death by nailing him to the cross. But God raised him from the dead, freeing him from the agony of death, because it was imposible for death to keep its hold on him . . .

'Exalted to the right hand of God, he has received from the Father the promised Holy Spirit, and has poured out what you now see and hear. For David did not ascend to heaven, and yet he said,

"The Lord said to my Lord:
Sit at my right hand
until I make your
enemies a footstool for
your feet."
Therefore, let all Israel be assured of this: God has made this Jesus whom you crucified both Lord and Christ.'

When the people heard this, they were cut to the heart and said to Peter and the other apostles, 'Brothers, what shall we do?' Peter replied, 'Repent and be baptised, every one of you, in the name of Jesus Christ so that your sins may be forgiven. And you will receive the gift of the Holy Spirit. The promise is for you and your children and for all who are far off — for all whom the Lord our God will call.'

With many other words he warned them; and he pleaded with them, 'Save yourselves from this corrupt generation.' Those who accepted his message were baptized, and about three thousand were added to their number that day.
Acts 2: 1-8, 12-17, 22-24, 33-41

many different languages of the pilgrims listening. Before this event they had been fearful of any opposition that they might encounter, but from now on they were willing to risk their lives in preaching and living out the teaching of Jesus.

Pictures of the Spirit in action

The New Testament gives us a number of graphic pictures of the Holy Spirit at work. Two of these pictures became a reality on the day of Pentecost, as Luke records:

Suddenly a sound like the blowing of a violent wind came from heaven and filled the whole house where they were sitting. They saw what seemed to be tongues of fire that separated and came to rest on each of them. Acts 2: 2, 3

What do these pictures of wind and fire, and a third picture of water, actually mean?

Wind

The image of the Spirit working as a violent wind was not new. In the Old Testament, the Hebrew word for 'spirit' was the word *ruach*. This word could also mean 'wind' or 'breath'. And as the air we breathe brings us life and vitality, so the Spirit brings

On the Day of Pentecost, as the Holy Spirit fell on the disciples, it seemed as though tongues of fire played round them. Fire in the Bible is a symbol of holiness and of the power of God in action.

us God's life; he makes us aware of God and gives us the energy we need to respond to him.

Ezekiel was sent a vision by God in which he saw a valley filled with human bones. God told Ezekiel to call on the wind to

66 **I will pour out my Spirit on your offspring, and my blessing on your descendants.** 99

breathe new life back into those who had died. This picture was to show that God was going to breathe new life and hope into those who had lost all confidence in him. In much the same way, the Holy Spirit brought new life to the disciples on the day of Pentecost.

Fire

John the Baptist once said about Jesus,

I baptize you with water for repentance. But after me will come one who is more powerful than I, whose sandals I am not fit to carry. He will baptize you with the Holy Spirit and with fire. Matthew 3: 11

This image of fire was used in the Old Testament to show the need for evil to be destroyed. Idols had to be destroyed by burning them, and metals were refined by fire.

The prophet Isaiah took this image of fire as something that destroys evil, and used it to show that God could take away a person's sins. In the same way, the Spirit took away the sins of the disciples and made them ready for the work God was to give them.

Water
John records that Jesus said,

Whoever is thirsty should come to me and drink. As the scripture says, 'Whoever believes in me, streams of life-giving water will pour out from his heart.'
John 7: 37, 38

Then John adds his comment:

Jesus said this about the Spirit, which those who believed in him were going to receive. John 7: 39

Water had often been seen in this way in the Old Testament – as refreshment from God. In a land that was short of good water supplies, this was a vital image. Jeremiah described God as a 'spring of fresh water', and Ezekiel said that God had promised to 'pour out' his Spirit on his people.

Forces for change
Wind, fire and water are all powerful forces for change in the world – whether they work violently, or in slow, quiet ways. So too the Holy Spirit is a force for change, as he brings God's power to work in our world.

How does the Spirit work?

Jesus did not give his disciples detailed teaching about how the Holy Spirit would continue the work that Jesus had begun. But the rest of the New Testament does tell us how the Spirit operates.

The fruit of the Spirit
Paul talks about the 'fruit' of the Spirit, that is, the effect the Spirit has on our behaviour as individuals. He lists these different qualities in this way:

The fruit of the Spirit is love, joy, peace, patience, kindness, goodness, faithfulness, gentleness and self-control.
Galatians 5: 22, 23

The teaching of Jesus is something we can regard as an ideal – and as we know, ideals are notoriously hard to live up to. But the Spirit fulfils the Old Testament hope that God would work inside us, helping us to do what he wants. This does not mean that we can sit back and do nothing, while God gets on with his work, but rather that we do not have to strive on our own. We work together with God in producing the fruit of the Spirit.

In Paul's list of the fruit of the Spirit, he is describing the sort of person Jesus was when he lived on earth. Jesus showed people love, he was patient with his followers and kind towards the weak. So as we grow as Christians these are the qualities that people begin to see in us. The work of the Spirit is to reproduce the life of Jesus in us. We become more like him.

Growth takes time

The fruit of the Spirit, like any fruit, takes time to grow and mature. Crops do not grow to maturity overnight. They need a year of careful planning and hard work before they can be made into useful food for us to eat.

At the start of the agricultural year, the hard ground is ploughed up, to make way for the sowing of seeds. The soil is fertilized, and as the crop begins to grow in the early spring, it will need to be rolled. Crop spraying takes place to protect the plants against insects. Gradually, over a period of months, with hard work and good weather, the grain will reach maturity – then it is ready for harvesting. When

THE SPIRIT AND THE CHRISTIAN

Cardinal Leon Joseph Suenens, until recently head of the Roman Catholic Church in Belgium:

The Holy Spirit was sent into the world after the ascension of Jesus to implement his own mission. Jesus told his disciples while he was still with them, that there were things they could not yet understand, but that the Spirit would teach them. Jesus only lived for thirty-three years, and was limited to his own country, but the Spirit continued his work on a world-wide scale.

The Holy Spirit was sent not to replace Jesus, but to accomplish and give the fullness of Jesus' presence. Jesus did *not* say, 'I am going away now — the Spirit will do my job!' No. Rather, he talked about

sending 'my' Spirit, the Spirit of 'my Father'. So the Holy Spirit really came to christianize Christians. But the real problem is, will Christians allow the Spirit to do this? Often people do not criticize us for being Christian, but for not being Christian *enough*. We need to allow ourselves to be moulded and filled by the Spirit, and to be emptied of ourselves.

Before we speak about the gifts of the Spirit, we need to speak about the Giver — the Giver is more important than the gifts. Once that has been clearly said, then we can stress the most important gifts of the Spirit — which are faith, hope and love. The Holy Spirit gives to each of us a special call. I would not say that he has a 'plan' for us, because the word 'plan' sounds rather like a computer,

already programmed. Rather, the Lord has a dream for each of us.

Every Christian is called to imitate some facet of the life of Jesus. We cannot represent every aspect at the same time. So one Christian is stressing, say, the love of the Lord for the poor — I think of Mother Teresa of Calcutta. Other saints are there to stress other aspects. So we work in a complementary way, and like a diamond that has the sun shining on it, we show Jesus in different facets. This is the work of the Spirit.

we see food on sale, it is easy to forget the time and effort that has gone into producing it.

In the same way, Christians only take on the character of Jesus as they grow in loving and following him. This is not something that happens instantly. The Holy Spirit, who gives us the fruit of patience, is himself patient with us in our growing, which is often slow.

The church needs the Spirit

Just as we need the work of the Holy Spirit as individuals, so too the church needs the Spirit. Without the Spirit, the church is like an army with no weapons. We may have our strategies and plans, our brilliant leaders and

❝ There are different kinds of spiritual gifts, but the same Spirit gives them. ❞

persuasive speakers, but if the Spirit is not working in these activities, we will achieve nothing. The Spirit equips the church for its work in the world. We cannot equip ourselves any more than an army can conjure up weapons out of nothing.

The apostle Paul compared the church to a body, each part functioning in harmony with the others. The Spirit has given different gifts to different members of the church, and only when each is using his or her gift properly does the body of Christ go into full action.

The Spirit not only gives life; he also unites the church. Even in the early days there were disagreements and arguments among church leaders. But there was still unity because the Spirit united the church in love. As soon as we lose sight of what the Spirit is doing in the church, there is bound to be bad feeling and disunity. So how does the Spirit work in the church?

The gifts of the Spirit

There are several passages in the New Testament that tell us some of the gifts that the Spirit gives to the church. They are called 'gifts' because they are given by God and are not merely talents or abilities that we have already. There is the gift of 'prophecy', where God speaks through someone to give guidance over a specific situation in the church. Or there is the gift of 'tongues', where people are free to praise God in languages they do not understand. There are also gifts of faith, healing, teaching and many others.

In one passage, Paul says that the church is like a human body which is made up of many different parts. In the church all these different abilities from God work together in strengthening the body of believers. And Paul goes on to say that these gifts are to be used carefully because those who make up the church love one another.

The gifts are not to be used selfishly, and they are not simply for the church to use for itself.

The church exists to continue Jesus Christ's mission – and the gifts are given to help the church in that work.

What is the work of the Spirit?

The activity of the Spirit showed up very clearly on the Day of Pentecost. The first thing that the newly-empowered church did was to preach to a crowd that had gathered, with the result that 3,000 of them were convinced and joined the church. From that time on, as the Spirit guided the direction of the church, the Christians were outward-looking, seeing their priority as spreading the good news. How does today's church measure up against this priority?

An obsession with tidiness
The church often works in the following way. Everything is well organized: we have our conferences, our doctrinal statements, our liturgies and traditions. Everything is well under control and running smoothly. Often the church has been more concerned to run itself as a well-oiled organization, instead of responding to the direction of the Spirit. But although we manage to make everything tidy inside the church, there is something missing. The atmosphere seems stale and heavy.

Opening the window
Then God opens the windows of the church and for a time we enjoy the breeze and the new life that it brings. But, like a breeze, the Spirit is unpredictable. He does not seem as concerned as we are for tidiness in the church. He begins to upset some of our cherished ideas and practices. Church leaders feel threatened because they are no longer in control – and so we close the window, and sadly the Holy Spirit is shut out of the church.

Either we have to learn to live with the idea that the church is to be run by God, or we shut the window and lose the vital work of the Spirit.

The Spirit of mission
When Jesus was alive on earth, he was often an uncomfortable person to be with. And so it can be with the Holy Spirit, who brings us into contact with Jesus. In many ways he can be very uncomfortable. He shakes us out of our rut. He disturbs our complacency. And he sends us out from the safety of our churches into the world. The

Holy Spirit is a Spirit of mission. He does not work to make us secure and comfortable *inside* the church, but to send us *outside*, to make new disciples of Jesus.

The Spirit in the book of Acts
We can see the Spirit working in this way in the book of Acts.

Jesus had told his disciples that they would be witnesses to him 'in Jerusalem, in all Judea and Samaria, and to the ends of the earth'. This meant they were to start their work in the city, then move out into the province of Judea and Samaria, and from there take the message of Jesus Christ all over the world. The

THE HOLY SPIRIT AND WITNESS TO JESUS

Michael Cassidy, founder of Africa Enterprise, explains how the Spirit has helped him to speak about Jesus Christ:

Right at the very beginning in the book of Acts, Jesus said, 'You will receive power when the Holy Spirit comes on you; and you will be my witnesses . . .' So from the very beginning Jesus linked the coming of the Spirit to his disciples with their being motivated to go out and share the message world-wide. I know that in my own experience, until Jesus became a reality to me in the Holy Spirit, I had little desire to tell anybody about him. But once the Holy Spirit was real in my heart, it was rather like in the book of Acts when the disciples said, 'We cannot help speaking about what we have seen and heard.' The Holy Spirit is given not just so that we may have

beautiful personal experiences, but so that we may be motivated to share the message of Jesus with the world around us.

And Michael Griffiths, (above) principal of London Bible College, says:

I think the central role of the Spirit is shown in the way that this frightened group of men were suddenly emboldened to go everywhere being witnesses to Jesus and his resurrection. This is a kind of enormous reversal. In

the Old Testament, the Jewish expectation seemed to be that the Gentile nations were going to come into Jerusalem to worship at the Temple. They would become like Jews in being circumcized and in not eating certain kinds of food. But in the book of Acts, the procedure is the other way around. Jerusalem is not the centre to which people come in, but the centre from which they go out under the guidance of the Holy Spirit. And it is this wonderful change from the inward movement to the outward one which I see as the overall work of the Spirit.

book of Acts is the story of this expansion and at each stage the Spirit was the person who pushed the early church further and further out, from Jerusalem as far as Rome itself.

So the Holy Spirit was not so much concerned to make the church into a good organization, but rather to mobilize it to spread the good news.

Moved by the Spirit

Throughout the history of the church there have been three main ways the Spirit and the church have related, or failed to relate. First, the church goes out into mission without the power of the Spirit, trying to do by its own efforts what only God can do. Second, the church enjoys the power of the Spirit, but refuses to use it by going out in mission, selfishly hanging on to the Spirit for its own experiences and enjoyment. Third, the church receives the power of the Spirit and is sent out into the world to proclaim Jesus.

These choices are still with us today. If the church is to grow and develop as God means it to, then we must follow the example of the early church in listening to the Spirit and allowing him to send us out into the society we live in.

Filled with the Spirit

Jesus once said, 'the mouth speaks what the heart is full of.' If someone carries a full glass and is jolted, what will spill out is whatever is in the glass. In the same way, as we are jolted in our daily lives, what will spill out of our mouths will be whatever we are full of. If we are full of greed or self-importance, we will not be

66 Do not get drunk with wine . . . instead, be filled with the Spirit. 99

able to help giving that away at moments of stress.

But if we are full of the Spirit, being changed by him to be more like Jesus, we will naturally communicate that to other people. Speaking about the good news of Jesus Christ is not something that we can manufacture. It should come naturally because we are full of Jesus, and full of the Spirit who sends us out. As the Spirit changes us, only then can he change others through us.

12
THE NEW AGE

How do we look at the future today?

From the earliest times, people have been fascinated by the future and have tried to control future events. The desire to know about and influence the future is still strong in twentieth-century society too. This is partly the reason why so many people take an interest in newspaper horoscopes, election predictions and even the weather forecast!

Thinking about the future can fill us with fear or excitement, depending on what kind of future we think we have. So how do we look at the future today?

Pessimism

There have always been prophets of doom who predict terrible things for the future. But today there is a general feeling among many people that the outlook for our future is bleak. The predictions of today's prophets of doom increasingly seem to be accurate. Our world faces a great number of problems and there is a shortage of solutions to them. Pessimists give good reasons for their existence.

Food supply

According to the World Bank, 780 million people today do not have enough money to buy the food they need. That figure is the equivalent of the combined populations of East and West Europe, North America, Japan, Australia and New Zealand. It would be the same as if the whole Western world, and more, was starving.

The Brandt Report, produced, not by prophets of doom, but by a committee including world statesmen, says that the gap between the rich and the poor is the crucial problem of our time. And this problem is not about to disappear. By the end of the twentieth century, the earth's population will have doubled its present number.

Arms spending

So how does our society respond to this horrifying statistic? The United Nations estimates that the amount the world spends on arms is $500 billion *each year*. That is twenty times the amount we spend on official aid to the poorer countries.

In addition 20% of the world's scientists do their research in the military area. This is the largest single area of scientific enquiry. There are more qualified scientists working on military research than there are working in agriculture, pollution control, health and energy *put together*. Clearly then, we consider defending ourselves against each other to be more important than feeding those who do not have enough food to live.

The overkill rate
The overkill rate is the term given to describe the number of times we are able to destroy every man, woman and child living today. Because of the immense destructive power of nuclear weapons, today we would be able to destroy ourselves no less than sixty times.

These statistics are well known, yet governments seem unwilling or unable to make any real progress in fighting the problems we face. So the pessimist gives us a very dark view of the future – if there is to be any future at all.

Optimism
However, there are optimists around as well, although they are far fewer than the pessimists. Today's optimist looks for solutions to our problems in improved technology and in the endless possibilities of outer space. He believes that the computer revolution will free people from tedious and boring jobs and enable them to live a more relaxed and fulfilling way

of life. Many of today's scientists are optimistic that scientific developments will lead us to an *improved* future, rather than into the nightmare that pessimists foresee.

> **❝ You were separate from Christ . . . without hope and without God in the world. ❞**

But this is not the view held by most people in Western society. In fact, it has been said that most young people today are not asking 'what does life mean?', but 'are we going to survive?'

How do people react to the future?
Many people react positively to the problems that confront us by trying to do something to change the situation. There is a great deal of popular involvement in politics, for example, and in campaigning to ban nuclear weapons.

But many more people react negatively and feel quite powerless in the face of the world's problems. And so they attempt to hide from the problems by deliberately turning their attention to other things. The enormous growth in the entertainment industry, through television, films, electronic games, sport and so on, reflects the degree of escapism present in society.

Are Christians optimists or pessimists?

The New Testament seems to contain a strange mixture of optimism and pessimism. On the optimistic side there is a heaven and so everything must work out all right in the end. But on the pessimistic side is some of the teaching of Jesus: *'Countries will fight each other; kingdoms will attack one another. There will be terrible earthquakes, famines and plagues everywhere; there will be strange and terrifying things coming from the sky.'* So what are Christians – optimists or pessimists?

Facing the facts

The Christian hope is not just in heaven, full stop. Often Christians have believed that and so have earned the criticism that they are 'so heavenly-minded that they are no earthly use'. Jesus in his teaching did not try to pretend there were no problems and neither should Christians today. And although Christians are called to be involved in working against the problems we face, the teaching of Jesus does seem to suggest that we are not going to be able to come up with any long-lasting solutions to our problems.

Beyond optimism and pessimism

Optimism is often little more than a vague hope that everything will somehow be all right in the end. It tends to ignore the problems we have. In that sense Christians are not optimists, because they have a firm hope that despite the real problems of the present God has not abandoned us, but will rescue us from our problems in the future.

While there is not a lot of hope for the world without God, there

❝ As in Adam all die, so in Christ all will be made alive. ❞

is a great deal to look forward to *with* God. We live in a world where most people see death as the worst possible thing that can happen to a person. But the Christian hope lies beyond death – in the resurrection. So the New Testament does not give us an optimistic or a pessimistic view of future events. It gives us reason to hope, because all of history is under the control of God.

Hope for the future based on the past

The New Testament hope for the future is a firm one because it is based on the character of a God who has shown that he can be trusted. Christians believe that God will act in the future because he has acted in the past. He has proved his reliability.

So what has God done that gives us reason to be hopeful about the future? The apostle Paul said:

We know that God, who raised the Lord Jesus to life, will also raise us up with Jesus and take us, together with you, into his presence. 2 Corinthians 4: 14

As God raised Jesus, so he promises to raise us from death when Jesus returns to wind up the affairs of history. If we are convinced that Jesus was actually raised, we can be equally convinced that God will

do as he has promised for us as well.

What kind of hope?

The New Testament picture of the future is quite different from the one that most people hope for. Many would prefer a future without God, and look for the solutions to the world's problems within history. And to talk about a hope *after* death makes grim reading in a world that believes that after death there is nothing.

But the teaching of Jesus was clear: there would be no solution to the problem of evil until history was interrupted and concluded by God. Without God there is no hope, but the New Testament teaches that God is at the end of history, and therefore there is hope. Peter captures this idea of God being ahead of us, preparing for us to be with him:

Let us give thanks to the God and Father of our Lord Jesus Christ! Because of his great mercy he

Our Christian hope is that Jesus will one day return. Will we be ready?

gave us new life by raising Jesus Christ from death. This fills us with a living hope, and so we look forward to possessing the rich blessings that God keeps for his people. He keeps them for you in heaven, where they cannot decay or spoil or fade away.

1 Peter 1: 3, 4

The second coming

Before leaving his disciples Jesus told them that he would one day return to the earth, not to live an ordinary human life again, but to raise the dead and call all people to face God's judgement. Jesus described it in this way:

Then the Son of man will appear, coming in the clouds with great power and glory. He will send the angels out to the four corners of the earth to gather God's chosen people from one end of the world to the other. Mark 13: 26, 27

Will Jesus return?

To many people such words of Jesus must seem rather like science fiction. Some have tried to explain Jesus' words by saying that he was not talking literally, but in a spiritual sense. In other words, Jesus was really saying that he comes again into our hearts as we believe in him. The problem with this sort of interpretation is that it turns a blind eye to many things that Jesus and the New Testament say about his return. They clearly saw it as the final event in history: one that would occur during a time of great trouble and distress. The second coming of Jesus is a vital element in the Christian hope for the future, and we have no more reason to doubt this teaching than any other part of the New Testament.

How should we prepare for the future?

The New Testament teaching about the future is not that we look forward to what we do not have at the moment. For the Christian, the present and the future are closely tied together. So before we look at how Christians should prepare for the future, we need to look at the way the present and the future affect each other.

The Jewish hope

When God's people in the Old Testament were attacked by other nations and taken away into exile, they looked forward to the time when they believed God

would return them to their land
and make them a great nation
again. However, this hope was
frustrated so many times that it
began to take on a new form.

By the time of Jesus the Jews
believed that God would send his
Messiah to interrupt history and
set up the kingdom of God. All
Israel's enemies and overlords
would be judged, and God's
people would live with him for
ever.

The New Testament hope

When Jesus came, his teaching
about the future was not quite so
simple. On one hand, he seemed
to be saying that the kingdom of
God was already here:

**Jesus went into Galilee,
proclaiming the good news of
God. 'The time has come,' he
said, 'The kingdom of God is
near. Repent and believe the
good news.'** Mark 1: 14, 15

On the other hand, he seemed to
say that the kingdom of God
would be in the future. At the
Last Supper he said,

**I tell you, I will never again drink
this wine until the day I drink the
new wine with you in my
Father's kingdom.**
Matthew 26: 29

Jesus wanted to show that the
kingdom of God would not
suddenly arrive as a complete
package, as the Jews were
expecting. Rather, he had come
to *start* the work of the kingdom

*The predictions Jesus made of wars and
disasters that would come before his return
have been fulfilled many times. His
promise is that into this world with its pain
and evil he will come back to bring God's
judgement and salvation.*

of God, but it would only come
fully when he returned. The
period of time between his
ascension and his return would
be an in-between period which
the Jews had not foreseen.
During that time, God's kingdom
would work in the middle of an
evil world.

Now, but not yet

So the kingdom of God is here
now (partially), but in another
sense it is *not yet* here (fully). So
the church lives in a time when

the kingdom of God is only partially at work. People respond to the good news, people are healed, and the Holy Spirit gives God's gifts to the church – all this shows that the kingdom is at work. But Christians also hope for the future coming of the kingdom, when we will live with God.

So Christians do not merely look forward to something they do not have at the moment. There is a real sense in which we already enjoy something of the future now. Our hope for the future means that we can work to bring some of the future qualities of the kingdom into our world now. We may work for a more just society, forgive those who wrong us, speak out on behalf of those who are disadvantaged. The kingdom of God is not merely in the future – it also invades the present.

Signs of the times

This whole period between Jesus' resurrection and his return is called 'the last days' in the New Testament. We should not think

THE LAST DAYS

Stephen Travis, author of the book The Jesus Hope, *explains how Christians should understand Jesus' teaching about his second coming:*

Some people would say that the Bible gives a detailed, blow-by-blow account of what is going to happen in the future. They will point to a passage such as Mark 13, where Jesus speaks about signs of the end, and say, 'Look, these things are happening in our own time, therefore Jesus was intending to say that the end is just round the corner.' Personally I do not think that is the way the passage is to be understood. When Jesus speaks about the signs of the times — false Messiahs, world disasters, persecution, and so on — he is saying, 'Do not be surprised that these things happen. Be warned. These are a part of what must take place. These are part of the conflict that goes on between good and evil.'

Jesus' teaching about the last days is something that Christians have to take seriously. First, because it is telling us what will happen. It is telling us about the coming of Jesus, about the leading of God's people into a new heaven and a new earth, and that ought to be important to us. It is not something we ought to be embarrassed about.

So the teaching about the future is first something that we should know about and rejoice in, but also it is something that should affect our lives. The teaching of the New Testament is not there just to titillate our brains. It is there to transform our lives, to give us perspectives by which to live. We are able to live in hope precisely beause we know that life does not come to a dead end, and the world does not come to a dead end, but God has a future for us. And that enables us to relax as we face the future with all its questions. In the safety which God has given us we can face the world, and we can work in the power of God to try to put into practice the values of God's kingdom — to work for righteousness, for peace, and for justice in society.

of 'the last days' as only the last few years before the return of Jesus. Many Christians think that the Bible is full of clues showing that there is a whole timetable of events leading up to his return. It looks as if all we have to do is tick the events off as they occur in history, and we will be able to pinpoint fairly accurately when Jesus should return.

But Jesus never meant his teaching to be used in this way. When he taught about his return, he was not merely giving information about the future. He meant his words to make his followers prepare for his coming by living properly in the present. The signs that he talked about – wars, famines, disasters and so on – were meant to characterize the whole period of the last days, and not only the last few years of that period. Because Jesus stressed the need to *be ready* for his coming, his parables on the subject are very practical and down to earth.

Being ready

Jesus once talked about a master who leaves his servant to go on a long journey. He gives his servant the responsibility of looking after his household. When he returns from the journey unexpectedly, the master will want to find that his servant has looked after the house and has treated his fellow servants well. In the same way, Jesus will judge us according to the way we have obeyed him in facing our responsibilities in this life.

Jesus said that we should be prepared for his coming, because it would come at an unexpected time, like the visit of a thief at the dead of night. To be prepared does not mean gazing upwards, forgetting our earthly responsibilities. Instead it means to fulfil those responsibilities.

How will God judge people?

The theme of God's judgement appears consistently throughout the Bible. Although judgement is an unpopular idea today, it is something we have to face up to. But how will God judge? What standards does he expect?

God's standard

Some people say that they are reasonably good people – better than some – and that they have done the best they can. But even if that were true, is it enough?

Jesus once gave some teaching about judgement known as the parable of the sheep and the goats. In this teaching, Jesus said that we will not be judged only according to any good or evil that we have done, but on the way we have responded to Jesus

> ❝ The Lord will bring to light the dark secrets and expose the hidden purposes of people's minds. ❞

himself. The sheep in the parable were different to the goats not only because they did different things, but because they were living out the character of Jesus. They were behaving in the way Jesus himself behaved when he lived on earth.

So Jesus is God's standard. When we measure ourselves up to the way that Jesus lived, we discover that we fall far short of what God expects of us.

Judgement starts now

But if God is going to compare us with Jesus, who stands a chance? No one does, if that is all there is to it. But because Jesus has

THE SHEEP AND THE GOATS

Jesus told a parable about Judgement Day:

When the Son of man comes in his glory, and all the angels with him, he will sit on his throne in heavenly glory. All the nations will be gathered before him, and he will separate the people one from another as a shepherd separates the sheep from the goats. He will put the sheep on his right and the goats on his left.

Then the King will say to those on his right, 'Come, you who are blessed by my Father; take your inheritance, the kingdom prepared for you since the creation of the world. For I was hungry and you gave me something to eat, I was thirsty and you gave me something to drink, I was a stranger and you invited me in, I needed clothes and

you clothed me, I was sick and you looked after me, I was in prison and you came to visit me.'

Then the righteous will answer him, 'Lord, when did we see you hungry and feed you, or thirsty and give me something to drink? When did we see you a stranger and invite you in, or needing clothes and clothe you? When did we see you sick or in prison and go to visit you?'

The the King will reply, 'I tell you the truth, whatever you did for one of the least brothers of mine, you did for me.'

Then he will say to those on his left, 'Depart from me, you who are cursed, into the eternal fire prepared for the devil and his angels. For I was hungry and you gave me nothing to eat, I

was thirsty and you gave me nothing to drink, I was a stranger and you did not invite me in. I needed clothes and you did not clothe me, I was sick and in prison and you did not look after me.'

They also will answer, 'Lord, when did we see you hungry or thirsty or a stranger or needing clothes or sick or in prison, and did not help you?'

He will reply, 'I tell you the truth, whatever you did not do for one of the least of these, you did not do for me.' Then they will go away to eternal punishment, but the righteous to eternal life.
Matthew 25: 31-46

made it possible through his death for us to receive God's forgiveness, those who accept this forgiveness will be judged by God as if they had met the standard he has set.

So as we believe in Jesus and live a life of active obedience to him, we are preparing ourselves to live with him after death. But if we turn from God in this life

66 You also must be ready, because the Son of man will come at an hour when you do not expect him. 99

and refuse to follow Jesus, we are preparing ourselves for a life without him after death. Judgement is not just something that happens to us in the future. It is something we are involved in now, by the choices we make in the present.

What happens after judgement?
In a court of law, after the judgement comes either release or punishment. So what comes after God's judgement? Jesus taught very clearly, as in the parable of the sheep and the goats, that at judgement all people will be divided into two groups according to the way they have lived in this life. One group will inherit the kingdom of God, while the other group will be sent out from God's presence.

How can a God of love do this?
The whole area of judgement is

extremely hard for us to accept, as it involves people. But there is a sense in which God, too, finds it hard. Jesus once grieved that God would judge the city of Jerusalem for rejecting his love. He said,

Jerusalem, Jerusalem! You kill the prophets, you stone the messengers God has sent you! How many times have I wanted to put my arms round all your people, just as a hen gathers her chicks under her wings, but you would not let me! Luke 13: 34

God is a God of love, and so he is grieved when people reject his love. It is because God loves us that he has given us the freedom to choose the way we should live. God's love is not like the love of a sleepy grandfather who simply wants everyone to enjoy themselves. He wants us to respond to his love, and make responsible choices in doing so.

God's justice
When people say that a God of love should not judge us, they overlook not only the quality of his love for us, but also that he is a God of justice too. Again and again the Bible tells us about God's justice: how he cares for those who are discriminated against, and is angry with those who oppress others. Often we see evil people getting away with the things they do, and we say 'there's no justice'.

But God's justice will be most perfectly displayed on the day of judgement, when finally justice will be seen to be done. Because God is just, he cannot simply close his eyes to the wrong things people have done in the past, any more than crime can go unpunished in a good society.

Judgement is up to us

It is easy to think of judgement as something that God does to us. We think of God banishing people from heaven, and ask 'How could he do such a thing?' But judgement is really something that we do to ourselves. We decide in this life whether or not we are interested in God. So we will include or exclude ourselves from God's presence. God will simply underline the choices we have made, and confirm our decision.

Hell

Some people have said, 'Well, if my husband has gone to hell, I want to go there to be with him.' But to say that is to misunderstand what hell means. To be in hell means to be isolated from all that is good and

66 This small and temporary trouble we suffer will bring us a tremendous and eternal glory. **99**

that we value in this life. There are many human qualities we take for granted that are God's gift to us: laughter, kindness, even our relationships. Hell is where these things are no longer given to us, because we have made it impossible for God to give any more. It is nonsense to think that we shall be reunited with anyone in hell, for hell is the place of separation and isolation. So we cannot talk about going to hell to 'be with' someone.

Heaven

Part of our difficulty in understanding judgement stems from a wrong idea we have about heaven. Many see heaven as the kind of place where all their desires, needs and dreams are fulfilled. It will be a place of continual enjoyment and relaxation. But the teaching of the New Testament is quite different.

Heaven is not a fantasy world arranged to suit our desires, but the place where we become fully human, as God has always intended us to be. It is the place where we serve each other rather than ourselves. We worship and love the God who has rescued us from sin. Heaven would be frightening and unbearable to the selfish, or to those who have no time for God or others.

The difficult belief

Belief in a hell is difficult, and in a sense it should be like that. It is remarkable that Jesus, who showed us more clearly than anyone the love of God, also told us more clearly than anyone about the judgement of God. He did this not to frighten us into believing, but because he loved us and wanted to warn people about the consequences of living without God.

We too must take hell seriously if we are to love people properly. If we love our non-Christian friend or neighbour, our desire will be to tell him or her about the Jesus who has made a way of escape from hell.

What is the Christian hope?

The Christian hope, first and foremost, is in God himself. Because we know God, and learn to have confidence in him, we know that what he has promised will be fulfilled.

The resurrection

Our hope is not for the release of our souls from our bodies, as many people imagine. The teaching of the New Testament is that at the last day, the day when Jesus returns, we shall be raised from death to be with God for ever. Paul expresses it in this way:

Listen to this secret truth: we shall not all die, but when the last trumpet sounds, we shall all be changed in an instant, as quickly as the blinking of an eye. For when the trumpet sounds, the dead will be raised, never to die again, and we shall all be changed. 1 Corinthians 15: 51, 52

A new heaven and earth

The final book of the Bible, Revelation, gives us a series of visions about the ending of history, the judgement, and what lies beyond. Near the end of the book, we read:

Then I saw a new heaven and a new earth. The first heaven and the first earth disappeared, and the sea vanished. Revelation 21: 1

The Christian hope is not that we will be taken up into some ethereal realm called 'heaven' (the 'new heaven' referred to here actually means a new sky), but that we will live on the new earth with God. If the word 'heaven' really means the presence of God, this means that we will enjoy heaven on the earth. Our hope is not for redemption *from* the world, but for the redemption *of* the world. God will re-create all things, and make them perfect as he did in the beginning.

The New Jerusalem

But not only will nature be restored, so too will humanity's relationship with God, and with others. There will be a city, the New Jerusalem, in this new creation. The city has always

Jesus taught that 'the Son of man' (his characteristic title for himself) would 'come with the clouds of heaven'. This means Jesus' second coming will not be in obscurity, like his first coming, but public and in majesty.

He (God) will settle disputes among great nations. They will hammer their swords into ploughs and their spears into pruning-knives. Nations will never again go to war, never prepare for battle again.

Isaiah 2: 4

been a symbol of mankind's communal life, and sadly it is in cities that human evil is most often seen.

But in this new city men and women live together in peace, working together and serving God together. This vision of the new city fulfils the picture that the prophet Isaiah had of Jerusalem. He says that people would come to Jerusalem to learn from God:

Jesus Christ is Lord

Jesus went through tremendous pain and suffering to bring about the restoration of creation and the reconciliation of people with God. Because Jesus has done all this, he has earned the right to the highest title in creation –'Lord'. Christians look forward to the time when all people will openly acknowledge his rule over all things.

'JESUS THEN AND NOW' VIDEO SERIES

Series Producer	Tony Tew	*Assistant to the Producer*	Beverly Eales
Drama Producer	Ann Kirch	*Music*	Dave Cooke
Drama Director	Hugh David	*Choreography*	Janet Randell
Studio Director	Andrew Quicke	*Title Design*	Philip Miles
Writer	Simon Jenkins	*Video Editor*	Steve Jagger
Programme presenter	Tina Heath	*Film Editor*	Richard Trevor
Research	Tim Dean	*Film Cameramen*	Jack Bellamy
Production/Research	Olave Snelling		Martin Lightening
Additional Research	Joanna Barlow		Pat Wood
	Susan Calland	*Original idea*	James Jones
	Jacqueline Clarkson		
	Maire Nic Suibhne	Recorded at CTVC Studios, Bushey.	

The Producer gratefully acknowledges the invaluable contribution made by the
following who acted as Editorial Advisors and Consultants:

Series Consultants
Dr David Cook
The Rev. David Field
Dr Dick France
Prof. I. Howard Marshall

Programme Consultants:
(who advised on selected programmes)
Prof. Sir Norman Anderson
Prof. R. J. Berry
Dr Donald English
Dr Michael Griffiths
The Rev. Tom Houston

The *JESUS THEN AND NOW* video
series is a Lella Video Production made
possible through the generous
sponsorship of The Trinity Trust.

Further information about the work of
The Trinity Trust, may be obtained from
their offices at:
57 Duke Street
London W1M 5DH
Tel 01 493 9827

ACKNOWLEDGEMENTS

Many of the photographs in this book
have been supplied by Lella Productions.
Additional photographs are reproduced
by permission of the following
photographers and agencies:

Barnaby's Picture Library, 32
Camera Press/Keston College, 124
J. Allan Cash Photolibrary, 23, 150
Keith Ellis, 115
Fritz Fankhauser, 79
Dr T. Gough/Christian Outreach, 73
Sylvester Jacobs, 55, 74

Lion Publishing/David Alexander, 9, 21,
26, 34, 51, 59, 77, 113, 141, 143; /Paul
Crooks, 13, 132: /Jon Willcocks, 35, 63,
65, 71, 84, 85, 94, 95, 109, 166, 179, 188
G. Moon/Frank Lane Agency, 163
David Morgan, 102
Popperfoto, 134, 140
Rex Features, 18, 29, 66, 110, 127, 129, 154,
181
Doug Sewell, 139, 175
Clifford Shirley, 37, 46, 88, 90, 147, 153
Topham, 81, 119
World Cup Collection, 97, 170
World Vision Picture Library, 101

J·E·S·U·S

THEN AND NOW

WORKBOOK

BY MAGS LAW

INTRODUCTION

This workbook section has been designed for individuals or groups to use with the book *Jesus Then and Now.* The notes can also be used alongside the video of the same title, produced by Lella Productions.

The questions and discussion ideas have been written:
● to help you to absorb and evaluate what you have read in the book or seen on the video;
● to help you to see for yourself what the Bible has to say about Jesus, and how what he said and did can relate to our lives today. This material can be used individually or by groups working together.

Using the Bible
It is vital to understand what the Gospels say, and not just work out our own ideas. So in each section references to passages or verses in the Bible are given. It does not matter which translation you use. There are several modern English versions, of which I would recommend the Good News Bible and the New International Version as the most readable and comprehensible.

When the reader is pointed to a passage or 'reference' in the Bible, it is given as follows: Matthew 13:44-46, which simply means Matthew's Gospel, chapter 13, verses 44 to 46.

Where single verses are given, it is usually helpful to read the verses just before and following that verse, so that you can see the situation or context in which the words were written or spoken.

After some of the questions, several references are given. It is usually not necessary to look up all these verses; one or two are often sufficient. The additional ones are given for those working in groups, or for those who are particularly interested in finding out more about that issue. The two main references are printed in bold type.

Some longer passages from the Bible, on which a whole section is based, are given under the heading 'read it yourself'. It is *not* necessary to read all these passages before you work through the section; they are there so that you know where to find them should you need to refer to them.

Using the video
If you are leading a small group using the video series of *Jesus Then and Now,* you should note the following points:

● View each programme and read the relevant section of the notes beforehand. Decide which areas your group would benefit from discussing.

● At the beginning of the video tape, set the counter on your video recorder to zero. Note the footage numbers for the start of any sequences you may wish to replay during the course of group study so that valuable time is not lost in searching the tape.

● Remember that video is not like live television. You can stop, go back, and take the programme at the pace best suited for your group. Occasionally the screen fades to black in some programmes, and these are designed as ideal points to stop the tape for thought or discussion.

Are there 'right' and 'wrong' answers?
Quite simply, this depends on the question! When you are answering the questions, it often helps to think them through in three stages: What do I think? What do I think the Bible says? What do other Christians say?

Often it is helpful to write down your answers to the questions and there are some pages at the back of the workbook which you can use for this.

Thought for action
Jesus' words and life demand a response from us — both a personal response to him, and a response in our actions. Many of the sections therefore include a suggestion for action. Don't limit yourself to these ideas; they are a jumping-off point rather than an end in themselves.

Jesus Then and Now, or Jesus Now and Then?
I hope that you will find the questions in this workbook both interesting and thought-provoking. While I was working on them, I once or twice made the mistake of referring to the book as 'Jesus Now and Then'! Perhaps that is what is lacking in our discipleship nowadays — we tend to include Jesus in our lives only 'now and then'. I hope that working through this book will help to make our discipleship a more continuous experience and our friendship with Jesus a more integral part of our lives.

Mags Law

1 BEGINNINGS

Why look at Jesus?

1 If someone asked you, 'Why should I bother to think about Jesus?' what reasons would you give them?

2 What made *you* decide to look at Jesus?
If you are working in a group, compare the reasons each of you would give for thinking about Jesus.

3 Have a look at what different people in the first century thought of Jesus and his influence. You will find some very different views in these verses: **John 6:66-69**; John 7:12; John 11:25-27; **Acts 5:27-40**; Acts 17:5-7; Acts 19:23-27.

4 Looking back from the twentieth century, what do you think of these reactions? Do people still react to Jesus in the same way?

How can we know about Jesus?

5 Why did the Gospel writers write their accounts of Jesus' life? Mark is brief and to the point:
'This is the Good News about Jesus Christ, the Son of God.' Mark 1:1.

Luke and John are more explicit. Read Luke 1:1-4, and John 20:30-31 and 21:24.

Why are there four different accounts?

6 Each of the four Gospels gives us a different view of the events of Jesus' life. This exercise will take you a little time, but it is well worth it.

Look at the story of the feeding of five thousand people. The four different accounts are in Matthew 14:13 21; Mark 6:30-44; Luke 9:10-17; John 6:1-14.

If you are looking at this in a group, ask four people to take the role of the four authors. Read the accounts out loud, in turn, and ask the 'authors' to point out the things they remembered, which are not in the other accounts. For example, John might say, 'I remember Jesus told us to collect up what was left so that it wouldn't be wasted.' (Only John's account records Jesus telling the disciples to do this.)

You can look at the accounts of Jesus' arrest in a similar way. The verses in brackets show some of the 'extra' details, which reflect the particular author's view of the events. Jesus' arrest is recorded in Matthew 26:47-56 (verses 53, 54, 56); Mark 14:43-52 (verses 51, 52); Luke 22:47-53 (verse 51); John 18:1-11 (verses 9, 10, 11).

For further discussion

7 Do you think the Gospel writers could have invented the story of Jesus' life? Do you think they *would* have done, bearing in mind all Jesus' teaching?

Into what kind of world was Jesus born?

(Omit this section if time is short.)

8 What were the main hopes and feelings of each of the different religious and political groups at the time of Jesus? *(Jesus Then and Now,* pages 14-19.)

9 From what you already know of Jesus, what in his teaching would have disappointed — and excited — each of these groups?

What do you think?

10 Does understanding the political, religious and geographical situation during Jesus' lifetime give us a better understanding of his teaching? If so, think of one particular way this knowledge is a help.

Why was Jesus' birth different?

Read it for yourself

11 Read Matthew 1:18-25 and Luke 1:5 — 2:40 and see how Jesus' birth was different:
   ● *different* in the way it came about (Jesus was not conceived through a normal, human sexual relationship);
   ● *different* in the special events surrounding it;
   ● *different* in its meaning.

Dig a bit deeper

12 Look at some of these verses, and see the meaning that the New Testament writers saw in the birth and life of Jesus: Colossians 1:15-20; Philippians 2:6-8; Hebrews 1:1-3; Hebrews 4:14, 15; John 1:14; Luke 2:25-35.

Think it over

13 Re-read the story of the birth of Jesus and, choosing one character, spend a few minutes trying to understand that person's feelings about what was happening.

For further reading
The New Testament Documents F. F. Bruce (IVP).
Christianity: the witness of history J. N. D. Anderson (IVP).

2 TEMPTATION

Who was John the Baptist?

Read it for yourself
The birth of John: Luke 1:5-25, 57-80
John's preaching: Luke 3:1-20; John 1:19-37; Matthew 3:1-12;
Mark 1:1-8.
1 What were the two main points of John's message?
2 What was John's practical teaching about the kingdom?

Jesus and the kingdom
3 Look at some of Jesus' teaching about the kingdom of God.
Remember that the Jewish people were hoping for a king to deliver
them from the Romans. Jesus plainly had a different kind of
kingdom in mind: Mark 1:15; Matthew 21:28-32; **Matthew 18:21-35;
Matthew 13:44-50;** Luke 14:15-24; John 18:33-38.
    Christians are to echo Jesus' prayer, 'May your kingdom come'.
So how does Jesus' teaching in these verses apply to our lives today?
4 Look at how working to bring God's rule into effect in the world
affected the lives of:
● Jesus: Matthew 3:13-15; Matthew 26:39, 42
● Mary: Luke 1:38
● Peter: Acts 4:18, 19; Acts 5:27-29
Does acknowledging Jesus' kingship in our lives affect us in the same
sort of way?

Repentance
5 Some Jews felt they had no need to repent because they were relying
on the fact that they were the chosen people. Matthew 3:7-9
What reasons do people give nowadays for saying they are not wrong
in God's sight?
6 Read Luke 5:30-32; Luke 6:41, 42
What do you think Jesus meant when he said these things?

Practical Repentance
7 Read Luke 19:1-9.
Do you agree with Graham Turner that for repentance to mean
anything it must involve positive action? (Replay the video or see
page 25 of the book).
    Are there some situations where to try to put things right would
cause more harm?
8 Think of Graham's situation and the four things he felt he had to
put right. What sort of arguments might he (or his friends) have put
up for simply stopping doing those things, but without trying to put
right the past?

Why did Jesus leave Nazareth?

9 What did baptism symbolize for John and his followers? Luke 3:3;
   Mark 1:4, 5
10 Now look at what Peter and Paul taught about baptism.
   Acts 2:38, 39; Romans 6:4; 1 Corinthians 12:13; Colossians 2:12
   What does Christian baptism represent?

Does the devil really exist?

11 Before you work through this section, stop and think, 'Do I believe
   that the devil exists as a personal being?' If you do, is it because:
   ● the Bible teaches that he exists?
   ● I know from my own experience?
   ● Jesus believed in his existence?
   ● I believe it from looking at the world around me?
   ● Some other reason?
   If you are working in a group, you could compare your reasons.
   Most people find it more difficult to believe in a personal devil that
   in some vague evil force. Why do you think this is?
12 What do you think is the wisest attitude for a Christian to take to
   the occult today?
   ● Ignore it?
   ● Keep informed so that you know what you are up against?
   ● Keep well away from anything to do with it?

What do Jesus' temptations teach us?

Read it for yourself
Matthew 4:1-11; Mark 1:12-13; Luke 4:1-13
13 In each of the temptations, the devil took some part of Jesus'
   ministry which was good, and tried to get Jesus to use this power in
   the wrong way. How do you think we can guard against being
   diverted in a similar way, and using our gifts and talents wrongly?

Jesus and us
14 Does it help to memorize verses from the Bible?
15 Look at Matthew 26:36-38.
   Jesus prayed, and wanted the support and companionship of his
   disciples. When we face temptation, do we pray, and are there
   Christians whom we feel we can ask for support?
16 Read Luke 22:31, 32; 1 Corinthians 10:13; Hebrews 7:35.
   How are these verses an encouragement to us when we face
   temptation?

3 DISCIPLES

Why did Jesus call the disciples?

Read it for yourself
Jesus calls the disciples Matthew 4:18-22; Matthew 9:9;
Mark 1:14-20; John 1:35-49

Quick facts to check on the disciples
1 Why did Jesus call the disciples? Mark 3:14, 15
2 Were their backgrounds similar or different? Mark 1:14-20; 2:13, 14
3 How did Jesus promise to help his disciples when he was no longer
with them? Matthew 28:20; Luke 21:14, 15; John 14:16, 17;
Acts 1:3-5, 8
   What did Jesus want from, and for, his disciples? Luke 9:23, 24;
Mark 3:31-35; Luke 21:34-36; John 17:6-26

Think it over
4 If we are disciples of Jesus, we can take what Jesus said and apply it
to our lives. Do we see Jesus' commands, and his prayer, coming
true in us?
5 The disciples gave up their jobs to follow Jesus. Did we give up
anything specific to follow him? Should we have done? If you have
used the video, think back to and discuss the drama sequence in
which the disciples argued over what the call of Jesus may have
meant for them.
6 When we doubt God's presence with us, or do not understand what
is happening in our lives, it can often help to see the disciples doubts
and fears. Look at one or two of these passages and see how Jesus
both understood and answered the disciples need: John 14:1-14;
Matthew 14:22-33; John 20:24-29

What does discipleship mean?

7 Try for a moment to put yourself in the place of someone, not a
Christian, who knows you. Ask yourself, 'Does . . . know I'm a
Christian?' Suggest to each other (or to yourself) some of the ways in
which your friend might know you follow Jesus. (Be honest!)
8 Generally speaking, what sort of things do people who are not
Christians use to identify a Christian? Do any of these phrases sound
familiar?
'He's religious . . . She goes to church . . . He doesn't swear . . .
She believes in the Bible and all that . . . He doesn't drink . . . He
hasn't got much sense of humour' (this sometimes, but not always,
means 'He doesn't laugh at dirty jokes') . . . 'She prays to God . . .
He doesn't fiddle the expenses . . . She's always talking about God.'

Now compare these statements with what Jesus said about being a disciple: Luke 14:25, 26; **Matthew 25:37-40;** John 14:23, 24, 27; **John 13:34, 35; John 15:11;** John 17:21-23
(For more of Jesus' teaching, look at Luke 6:27-38)

It's too difficult

9 Even when people see in us the qualities that Jesus said we should show, there will still be opposition. What do Jesus' example and teaching tell us about how we should react to unwarranted criticism and opposition? **Luke 12:4-7, 11, 12;** Matthew 5:10-12; **John 16:33;** John 17:14, 15

10 One of the twelve apostles, Peter, wrote in his letter to some fellow-Christians about the suffering that disciples of Jesus must be prepared to face. You can read what he wrote in 1 Peter 2:21-23 and 1 Peter 4:12-16. Notice that Jesus and Peter are talking all the time about opposition that comes as a result of following Jesus. Are there some sorts of opposition and suffering that we bring on ourselves? (See also Margaret Dehqani-Tafti on the video or on page 50 of the book.)

Sometimes it seems that the hardest part of discipleship is living with other disciples! Even Jesus' close friends didn't always get on with each other. Read Mark 10:35-45 and Mark 9:33-37. We are often so sure we are right! Jesus' first disciples were just the same. Look at Mark 10:13-15 and Matthew 16:21-23. It's worth remembering these incidents next time we are sure we know best.

What effect does discipleship have?

Salt and Light

11 Jesus said his disciples (that's you and me!):'**You** are the light of the world . . . **you** are the salt of the earth.' (Delia Smith explains some uses of salt on the video.) Can you think of at least one way in which your life as a disciple of Jesus can be salt . . . and light:
- in your home?
- in your place of work, or school?
- in your leisure activities?

Making disciples

12 Read these verses first: 1 Thessalonians 5:14; 2 Timothy 2:2. Discuss with others (or think over yourself) the four steps in discipling suggested in *Jesus Then and Now,* page 49.

In what areas of your Christian life do you think these steps could help you?

13 Do you agree with the four steps suggested? Are they put into practice in your local group of Christians? If not, how could they be?

14 Are there any principles about working with others that we can learn from the way Jesus sent out his disciples? Look at Mark 6:7-13 and Luke 10:1-12.

4 MIRACLES

Why is there pain and suffering?

Read it for yourself

1 God made a plan: **Genesis 1:26-31;** Psalm 8:1-9; Psalm 115:15-16
  but mankind rebelled: **Genesis 3:6-13;**Isaiah 53:6; Romans 1:20-23
  This rebellion has spoiled relationships: **Genesis 4:1-10;** James 4:1;
  Amos 5:10-12
  and deeply marred our world: **Genesis 3:17-19;** Isaiah 24:4, 5
  Did Jesus promise that his followers would be spared suffering?
  Look at Mark 13:5-13, and see Godfrey Williams on the video or
  page 62 of the book.

2 The writer of Psalm 73 knew what it was to suffer without knowing
  the reason:

> When my thoughts were bitter
> and my feelings were hurt,
> I was as stupid as an animal,
> I did not understand you.
> Yet I always stay close to you,
> and you hold me by the hand.
> You guide me with your instruction
> and at the end you will receive me with honour.
> What else have I in heaven but you?
> Since I have you, what else could I want on earth?
> My mind and my body may grow weak, but God is my strength;
> he is all I ever need. *Psalm 73:21-26*

Read the rest of the psalm for yourself. What emotions does the
writer feel? What are the things that encourage him?

Act it out

3 If you are working in a group, one or two members could take the
  role of people who are not Christians, and challenge the rest of the
  group with these questions:
  Why do the innocent suffer, if God is a God of love?
  Why does God allow suffering? Can't he stop it?
  Why don't Christians do more to stop suffering? All they do is
  preach about accepting it bravely!
      The two people taking on the questioning role need to be ruthless
  and not accept terms or explanations they don't understand.

Prayer and action

4 Pray that God will show you a practical way in which you can help
  to relieve the suffering of some in your immediate community, and in
  other parts of the world — and then do something about it.

Why did Jesus work miracles?

A quick language lesson!
The English word 'miracle' is used for three different words in Greek (the language the Gospels were written in):
● 'mighty works' − effectiveness, or power;
● 'wonders';
● 'signs', with deep significance.

5 In our 'scientific' age most people think that miracles are above (or even against) the natural laws of the universe, as if, in miracles, God is 'interfering' with the natural order. At the back of our minds we often make the mistake of thinking of God as setting the universe to work like a piece of machinery. But the Bible always shows God in a living and personal relationship with his creation.

Discuss with each other what you think about miracles. Do you believe they happen? What is happening when a miracle occurs? What part does faith play?

6 Some people today try to 'explain away' what Christians would call miracles by saying 'it's all psychological' (as with healing, for example) or 'it's just coincidence'. What would be your response to this?

The miracles of Jesus
Look at one or two of the miracles Jesus performed, as in Luke 5:18-26 or Luke 13:10-17. See if you can answer these questions:
7 Why did Jesus work this miracle?
8 Was it easy for Jesus to work miracles?

Do the miracles prove who Jesus was?

9 Look again at the miracle stories in Luke. What was the effect of this miracle on the people there at the time?
10 In what way was this miracle significant − a sign pointing to who Jesus was?
11 Did the miracles prove to people who Jesus was?

Find it hard to believe?
If you find the question of miracles difficult, it's well worth doing a bit of homework. For example look at the entry on 'Miracles' in *The Lion Handbook of Christian Belief*.

Miracles today?

12 If someone who is ill were to ask you, 'Should I ask God to heal me?', what would you say?

5 LIFESTYLE

How did Jesus live?

Look at Luke 9:57-62

1 Jesus gave up a secure, well-paid job for an uncertain, dangerous life. Does this mean we should do the same?
2 Jesus depended on the hospitality and support of his sympathizers. Are all his followers called to do this? See Luke 8:3 and Ephesians 4:28.
3 We have seen that Jesus and many of his followers sacrificed their financial security, even their social popularity. How important to you is:
   ● financial security?
   ● social acceptance?
4 Some Christians lose one or both of these through, for example, unemployment, not necessarily as a direct result of following Jesus. How hard would you find it to cope with losing these two things? Do you think you would feel differently, depending on what caused the loss?
5 Jesus knew no 'us' and 'them' (look at Luke 7:36-39). His disciples had to learn the same lesson (Acts 10:19-35, 45). In what practical ways can we follow this example of Jesus today?
6 In *Jesus Then and Now* (page 68) Jean Vanier says, 'I think the most important thing is for us all to say . . . "How can I, today, at my home, in my little community life, my family life, become open to a rejected person?" '
   Think about this for a few moments in practical terms. For example: Should Christians be more prepared to be foster parents? What about our attitude to, and involvement with, mentally handicapped people? . . . those in prison? . . . prostitutes? What about our reaction to those at school, or work, who are unpopular?

What did Jesus teach about lifestyle?

Inner Change

7 Read these verses: **Mark 7:14-23; Matthew 23:25-28;** Luke 16:15; 1 Samuel 16:6, 7
   Ask yourselves, 'What inner changes has God made in me? What outward effect have these changes had?'
8 What other changes do you think God wants to bring about in you?

How should we live?

9 What do you think the main pressures of our consumer society are?
10 Replay the video of Ronald Sider or read the section 'Christian

Action for the Poor' (page 76 in *Jesus Then and Now*). Do you agree with what Ronald Sider says?

11 Do you think his suggestions could work, in practical terms?

12 Which of the suggestions, if any, do you think could be tried in your local fellowship, or among a smaller group of local Christians?

13 Read Jesus' words in Luke 14:12-14. Whose home was Jesus eating at? (Look back to verse 1 of the chapter.)

14 Should we take what Jesus says here literally, next time we hold a party? If not, why not? (If you think this is one isolated saying, look at Luke 6:32-38.)

15 Does what Jesus says make us uncomfortable?

16 Did he really mean us to do what he says?

Take up the challenge

17 *As a group.* Decide on one positive change you could make in your life style (either as individuals or through group action) to reflect Jesus' teaching more closely. Think about the practical details, the possible snags, and the commitment needed. Then **do it** — don't just talk about it!

18 *Individually.* Think through what you have learnt about Christian lifestyle and see if there is a particular attitude you hold which you feel God wants to change. Make changing this attitude a point to think, pray and act on over the next few weeks.

Words to remember

'Instead (of worrying about food and clothes) . . . be concerned above everthing else with the kingdom of God and with what he requires of you, and he will provide you with all these other things.'
Matthew 6:33

6 PRAYER

What is Prayer?

Think It Over

1 How would you answer someone who said that prayer is just a psychological trick?

2 What did Jesus teach his disciples to call God? Look at Luke 11:1, 2.

Prayer is a relationship with God our Father

3 Think of your closest friend and the relationship you have with him or her. Ask yourself:
  ● What do I give to the relationship?
  ● What do I receive from the relationship?
  ● What makes this friendship a good one?
(It may help you to think more clearly if you write down some ideas.)
Now take your answers one at a time and ask:
Do I see these things in my relationship with God?
If not, how can prayer help me to begin to develop them?

4 If you are studying this book in a group, ask each person what he or she finds to be the most important thing about prayer, and which aspect of prayer is the most difficult. Share some of the things which each person has found a help in praying, and some of the ways that prayers have been answered.

What can Jesus teach us about prayer?

5 'Christians believe that prayer changes people and events, and not only the one who prays.' (*Jesus Then and Now,* page 82) Look again at the occasions when Jesus prayed. If we followed Jesus' example for each of these occasions, how might prayer both help us **and** change events?
  ● Early in the morning Mark 1:35
  ● Before big decisions Luke 6:12, 13
  ● Facing temptation, and situations difficult to understand Matthew 26:36-41
  ● Needing encouragement or strength Luke 3:21, 22; Luke 5:16
  ● Concern for others Luke 22:31, 32; John 17:20, 21
Read the section 'There are no rules in prayer' on page 88 of the book, and discuss.

Why is prayer so difficult?

6 Ask yourself why, and when, you find prayer most difficult.
  Do any of these reasons sound familiar?
  ● When I feel it to be a duty.

- When I know I haven't obeyed God.
- I don't feel the need to pray.
- When I haven't prayed much recently.
- When my prayers don't seem to be answered.

Do you have other reasons?

How can we solve these kinds of difficulty?

7 If we see prayer as part of our relationship with God, should we expect it always to be easy?

How can we develop in prayer?

8 David Watson and Simon Jenkins suggest six things that will help us to develop in prayer. (*Jesus Then and Now,* pages 92-96)

Each of these six things could be applied to building any friendship. We could spend a long time studying Jesus' approach to prayer, or discussing the subject of prayer with others, neither of them good substitutes for getting on with praying and building our friendship with God. So, taking each of the six suggestions, write down a way of putting each into practical effect in your life. Take another look at your notes in a week's time and see if you have started doing these things.

An example would be: Sometimes when you are talking to a friend, remember that Jesus is in on the conversation. If there is an empty seat, think of it as where he is sitting.

Replay the video (or read page 93 of the book); where Metropolitan Anthony of Sourozh speaks on prayer. He stresses the need to prepare ourselves for prayer. Do we tend to approach God without realizing who he is?

More about prayer
Luke 18:1-14; Matthew 6:5-15; Luke 11:1-13; Romans 8:26, 27;
James 5:13-18; Hebrews 4:15, 16; Colossians 4:2-4

Further reading
Prayer is for You, by Graham Claydon (available from ISCF, 130 City Road, London, EC1V 2NJ, 40p).

7 THE MAN

What kind of person was Jesus?

The wrong people

1 Why was it so shocking to the Jews to see Jesus eating with tax collectors?

2 What other people did Jesus mix with? Look at **Luke 7:1-9, 31-35; Luke 8:1-3, 40, 42**; Luke 5:12, 13; Luke 14:1

3 With whom do you think Jesus would be spending his time, if he was living in your town today?

4 Why was Jesus prepared to break the social rules of his time? Read Luke 5:30-32; Mark 6:34

5 From reading some of the following verses, what sort of things do you think made Jesus angry or sad? **John 2:13-17; Luke 11:46, 52; John 11:32-36**; John 13:21

6 What sort of things should Christians be angry about today? Do you think they should be more concerned with social injustice than with individual sin?

7 Spend a few moments thinking quietly about whether there is anything in the way you live which would sadden or anger Jesus.

8 'When we listen to what Jesus said about himself, we hear things that no one in his right mind would dream of saying unless they were true.' (*Jesus Then and Now*, page 108)
Look again at some of the things Jesus said: **Luke 5:20-26; John 10: 25-33**; John 11:25, 26; Mark 14: 61-64; Luke 22:19, 20
What would be your reaction if someone you knew said things like this to you? What were people's reactions at the time?

9 Peter knew Jesus better than anyone. What did he think?
'Jesus is the one of whom the scripture says, "The stone that you despised turned out to be the most important of all." Salvation is to be found through him alone; in all the world there is no one else whom God has given who can save us.' Acts 4:11, 12. See also Acts 2:22-24 and 1 Peter 2:22. So we see that Jesus' life backed up what he said about himself.

Who did Jesus say he was?

10 Look again at 'Jesus tells us who he is' (page 105 in *Jesus Then and Now*). Ask yourself, 'In what way does Jesus, the bread of life, satisfy my hunger?'. John 6:25-35

11 'A branch cannot bear fruit by itself; it can only do so if it remains in the vine . . . Whoever remains in me, and I in him, will bear much fruit.' John 15:4, 5
Do we accept that, to achieve anything for Jesus, we need to be

totally dependent on him, like a branch on a tree, or do we try to do things in our own strength?

12 How can we make sure we 'remain in' Jesus (stay attached to, and dependent on, him)?

13 What sort of thing do you think Jesus meant when he talked about us 'bearing fruit'?

Who is Jesus?

How would you answer?

14 What would you say in reply to someone who said, 'I think Jesus was a good man, and a good moral teacher, but his disciples were deluded when they thought he was God.'?
(Note. Muslims claim that Jesus never said he was God, and that the Bible has been changed in this respect.)

15 How would you answer this argument?
'Anyone can claim to be God. It doesn't mean it's true.'
(Members of the Unification Church – 'Moonies' – claim that Jesus failed in his mission, and that Rev. Moon is the new Messiah.)

16 Why do you think people prefer to think of Jesus as simply 'a good man' or 'a good teacher', even though this doesn't make sense when we look at what he actually claimed?

17 Is it enough for us to say, 'Yes, I accept the fact that Jesus was the Son of God'? Is there more to being a Christian than just saying we believe it?

8 OPPOSITION

Why was Jesus arrested?

Read it for yourself
The accounts of Jesus' arrest and trial are in: Matthew 26:47 –
27:26; Mark 14:43 – 15:15; Luke 22:47 – 23:25; John 18:1 – 19:16

A quick check on the facts
1 You will find the answers to these questions in Mark 14 and
Luke 23:1 5.
  ● Who wanted Jesus arrested?
  ● Where did they plan to arrest him?
  ● Who helped them, and how?
  ● Did Jesus resist arrest?
  ● What happened when the Jewish authorities tried to get witnesses
to Jesus' 'crimes'?
  ● What charge did the Jewish (religious) authorities find him guilty
of?
  ● What was the penalty for this under Jewish law?
  ● What charges did they bring against Jesus when they took him to
the Roman (civil) authorities?
  ● Did Pilate find Jesus guilty?
  ● Why didn't he release Jesus?
  ● Whose release did the crowd ask for?

How is Jesus opposed today?

2 Do you think Christians in your own society face opposition today?
  If you do, what forms do you think this opposition takes? If not,
  why do you think there is little opposition?
3 'We fail to follow the Jesus who rocked the boat and put people's
  backs up over the real abuses in society.' (*Jesus Then and Now,* page
  121)
  What do you think are the 'real abuses' in society today
  ● in your local community?
  ● in the wider world?
  Do you think Christians say and do enough to oppose these wrongs
  in society? Do you do anything about them?

The kingdom of God
4 'If one of you wants to be first, he must be the slave of all.'
  Mark 10:44
  Compare what Jesus said here with Matthew 5:38-42.
  Does this mean we should let people 'walk all over us'?
  Read James 2:1-9.

Prejudice in ourselves is really hard to detect, because we always seem to be able to find apparently good, logical reasons for our attitudes. Also, prejudice may remain hidden until something happens to bring it out into the open.

Ask yourself these questions:

5 Are there certain people, or groups of people, in my neighbourhood whom I try to avoid, so simply never bother to become involved with?

Why is this?

6 Does my local fellowship of Christians reflect the make-up of the neighbourhood: rich and poor, black and white, employed and unemployed, young and old? If not, why doesn't it? Does what we say or do, or how we do things as a fellowship suggest to the neighbourhood that church is only for certain types or classes of people?

7 'The world should look at us and see we are different. We are meant to be God's alternative society.' (*Jesus Then and Now,* page 125)

In an earlier section we looked at the difference there should be in the way we live as disciples. Do we feel that the people around us could look at our local fellowship and see something of God's pattern for an alternative society?

If not, what are we doing about it? Do we tend to blame everyone else in the church? Do we try to force our ideas on the rest of the fellowship? Do we look for another church? Or what can we do?

Feeling the pressure

8 Ridicule, apathy, or being given the cold shoulder because of our Christian faith very quickly wear down our patience and our love. This is especially so if we daily face a situation where we are the only Christian. How can we cope with this?

9 Think of the pressures that Martin Luther King and Oscar Romero, or Festo Kivengere, experienced. Is there anything we can learn for our own situation from how they responded? (See the video or pages 122, 125, 126 of the book.)

10 Whether or not you are in this sort of situation, try to think of another person in your group who may be, and remember to pray for him or her. There may be practical ways you can help – perhaps meeting such a person at lunchtime, to pray or just to have lunch and talk!

9 CRUCIFIXION

Why is the cross central to Christianity?

The cross as a symbol

1 What did a cross mean in the time of Jesus?
2 How do you think people view the cross as a symbol nowadays?
3 Why do people wear them?

Act it out

4 If someone is wearing a cross, there can be an opportunity to share the good news of Jesus with them. You may like to try a role-play with two people. One takes the role of a Christian and the other of someone who is not a Christian, but always wears a cross. Here is how a conversation might go:

'Is that gold, that cross you're wearing?'
'Yes, it's nice, isn't it? My boyfriend bought it for me.'
'Why do you wear a cross? Do you think it means anything special?'

Discuss the conversation afterwards, and decide whether the 'Christian' was tactful or offensive, understandable or bewildering.

5 Read what Paul said about the cross in 1 Corinthians 1:17-25. Do you think people today are more likely to find the cross 'offensive' or simply 'nonsense'?

Peter, who spent so much time with Jesus, was in no doubt as to what the cross meant:

'For Christ died for sins once and for all, a good man on behalf of sinners, in order to lead you to God.' 1 Peter 3:18

What is sin?

6 Many people today do not believe in 'absolute' right and wrong. They see everything as 'relative'. This means, in effect, that something may be 'good' in one situation and 'bad' in another. Christians believe that God has absolute standards of right and wrong, however hard they sometimes are to work out in practice. The Jews of Jesus' time would have accepted this completely. Usually, people only believe in absolute right and wrong if they also believe in the existence of God.

How would you answer people who say:
'Who are you to say what's right and what's wrong?'
'I've never done anyone any harm.'
'God's just a killjoy. He doesn't want us to enjoy ourselves.'
'I can't help the way I am – I'm only human.'

These passages from the Bible may help you: Isaiah 59:1-4, 8-15; Romans 3:9-20

You could also look at Hosea 7:1, 2; Deuteronomy 7:7-11; 8:5, 6; Mark 2:7

7 We can easily deceive ourselves about what sin is, and its effect on us. Often we gloss over what is wrong with us, but are very good at seeing what's wrong with other people. Jesus pointed to this on many occasions.

Look at Luke 6:37-42. There is plenty of evidence for Jesus' sense of humour in this brief picture! If you have some creative minds in your group you may like to work out a brief dramatization of what Jesus said.

How is Jesus' death a solution to sin?

Read it for yourself
The story of the Passover is in Exodus 11:1 − 12:28. (You might like to replay David Watson's explanation of the first Passover on the video.)

8 Do you find the idea of sacrifice difficult to understand?

9 Try to think of examples where someone has sacrificed (given up) something for others.

10 Recently an old man who was unable to pay his rates was jailed − and then freed the following day because an anonymous well-wisher paid his fine for him. Is this an accurate picture of how Jesus' death is a solution for our sin? Read Romans 5:6-11 and see Paul explain how Jesus' death has solved our estrangement from God.

What did Jesus' death achieve?

11 Jesus saved us by his death on the cross. Have we experienced the meaning of this salvation in our own lives?

Look in turn at each of the pictures of what Jesus has done for us, and then think over how you have experienced being set free, put right, reconciled.
These verses may help to understand:
set free, bought back, redeemed − Ephesians 1:6-8;
Colossians 1:13, 14
put right, justified − Colossians 2:13, 14; Romans 4:25 and 5:1, 9
reconciled, made God's friends − 2 Corinthians 5:19, 20;
Colossians 1:21, 22

A thought for action
12 Jesus has reconciled us to God, and made us his friends. So have we tried, through our words and actions, to be reconciled to those who have something against us?

10 RESURRECTION

Is the resurrection important?

Read it for yourself
Matthew 27:57 – 28:15; Mark 15:42 – 16:8; Luke 23:50 – 24:49;
John 19:31 – 21:24
1 In *Jesus Then and Now,* the question is asked, 'Is the resurrection important?' What do you think?

Did Jesus really rise from death?

2 If someone challenges us to 'prove' the resurrection of Jesus, it can sometimes help to ask them about other things that they believe in, and why.
    For example, try asking yourself – or someone else: Do you believe America exists? Do you believe deeply enough to get on a plane and go there?
    Compare the reasons given with the reasons for believing in the resurrection, and look at the extent to which trust, or faith, leads to belief beyond reasonable doubt.

Is it hard to believe?
Read John 20:24-29
3 If you are working in a group, discuss honestly any aspect of the resurrection story which you find it hard to understand or accept. If you are using this book on your own, write down any queries you have and talk them over with another Christian, or read one of the books suggested at the end of this section.
    Either Christianity is based on truth, or it is a lie. You can read what Paul said about this in 1 Corinthians 15:12-19.
4 One of the strongest pieces of evidence for the resurrection is the dramatic change in the disciples. See their state of mind before it happened: Mark 14:50 and 16:8; John 20:1, 2, 19 . . . and after: Acts 4:13-22 and 5:40-42.
Note the difference!
What difference does it make to our everyday lives that Jesus is alive?
5 Take one or two of the following statements, which might be made by someone not prepared to accept the resurrection, and decide how you would answer them.
    ● 'Jesus didn't actually die on the cross. He just passed out and then recovered in the tomb.'
    ● 'I think it was all wish-fulfilment. The disciples wanted to believe Jesus wasn't really dead, and so they had hallucinations about him being alive.'

- 'I reckon the disciples stole Jesus' body so that they could say he'd risen from the dead. That's what the authorities said at the time, isn't it? It's in the Bible.'
- 'The resurrection? Well, the disciples made a mistake, didn't they? They went to the wrong tomb, found it empty, and jumped to the conclusion that he'd come back to life.'
- 'Well, I think "intelligent" people don't really accept the physical resurrection of Jesus. I think the resurrection story is symbolic.'

6 If you're not sure how to answer some of these objections, replay the video sequence in the judge's chambers, or read through pages 145-155 of the book again. What other objections do people raise to believing in Jesus' resurrection?

What does the resurrection mean?

7 Look at some of the apostles' preaching in the early days of the church. What meaning did they see in the resurrection?
Read Acts 5:27-32; Acts 13:29-39

8 In *Jesus Then and Now,* David Watson and Simon Jenkins point to two things that the resurrection establishes (pages 156-57). What are they? Perhaps you can remember without turning back to the book? Here are two 'clues': What does 'vindicate' mean? Who, or what, has been defeated?

9 How does the resurrection of Jesus affect our attitude to death?

For further discussion

10 Read 1 Corinthians 15:35-58. What question is asked, and how does Paul answer it?

If you want to read more about the evidence for the resurrection, these two books are excellent:
Who Moved the Stone? by Frank Morrison (Faber), described as 'the inner story of a man who originally set out to write one kind of book and found himself compelled by the sheer force of circumstances to write quite another'.
Verdict on the empty tomb, by Val Grieve (Falcon) — a lawyer looks at the facts.

11 THE SPIRIT

Read it for yourself
The ascension: Acts 1:3–11
The coming of the Spirit: Acts 2

A quick check on the facts
1 When, in relation to the resurrection, did the ascension happen?
2 What particular groups of people did Jesus appear to in this period?
3 What did Jesus do, and talk about, in the period between his resurrection and ascension?
4 What did he promise the disciples before he left them?

Can we believe in the ascension?
5 Do you find the ascension hard to believe or understand? If you do, discuss it with the group, or with another Christian.
6 What did the disciples believe had happened to Jesus?
Look at: Acts 2:33; 3:21; 5:31; 7:55, 56

Who is the Holy Spirit?
7 What was the work of the Spirit of God in Old Testament times?
(See page 162, *Jesus Then and Now*)
Here are some references to the work of the Spirit in the Old Testament: Genesis 1:2; Exodus 31:1-5; Numbers 11:23-29; 1 Chronicles 12:18; 2 Chronicles 15:1, 2; Psalm 104:30; Ezekiel 11:5
8 What did God promise to do in these two messages he gave to Ezekiel and Joel? Ezekiel 36:26, 27; Joel 2:28-32

Pictures of the Spirit in action
9 Imagine yourself in a situation where you long for:
- a breeze or wind;
- fire;
- water.

How are these situations like the work the Holy Spirit does in the life of a Christian? You might like to replay the video sequence at the watermill for a vivid picture of the Spirit in action.
10 Wind, fire and water are powerful forces and sometimes, in the physical world, we do not welcome their influence. As well as bringing comfort and refreshment, the Holy Spirit can be an uncomfortable influence in our lives. Can you think of examples where the Holy Spirit's work in your life could be (or has been) a disturbing experience?

How does the Spirit work?
11 What did Jesus tell his disciples about the work of the Holy Spirit?

Look at John 15:26; John 16:8, 13-15; Luke 12:11, 12.

12 See if you can find from these verses at least five ways in which the Spirit works.

Think for a few moments and then write down any particular areas of your life (personal or social) in which you feel you need the help of the Holy Spirit at the moment.

Next look at these verses and make a note of how the Spirit works in us: Romans 8:5, 15-17, 26, 27; Galatians 5:22, 23; 2 Corinthians 3:18

Now compare the two lists you have made, and spend some time thinking and praying over the way the Spirit can help.

(If you are watching the video, replay the part where Ian Petit speaks of cherries on a tree or bricks in water.)

What is the work of the Spirit?

13 Look at these two passages to see what is the Holy Spirit's work in the church (or fellowship of Christians): 1 Corinthians 12:4-7; Ephesians 4:2-7.

Do you think Christians today are guilty of neglecting either the gifts of the Spirit or the unity that the Spirit wishes to bring?

Filled with the Spirit

14 Imagine − or actually carry out − the following idea. (Doing it will make it stick in your mind much better!) Take a small glass or cup and fill it absolutely full to the brim with water. Carry it across the room and put it down. You'll find it very difficult not to spill any!

Sit down and re-read 'Filled with the Spirit', on page 174 of *Jesus Then and Now*. What can you learn from your action (carrying the full glass) about being filled with the Spirit? (Note. A lively alternative demonstration, which may produce other insights into the work of the Spirit, if you are working in a group, is to have a well-shaken bottle of lemonade handy.)

12 THE NEW AGE

Are Christians optimists or pessimists?

1 What are your feelings about:
- your future?
- the future of the world?

2 What are the things you fear most about the future?

3 Do you feel there is anything we can do to solve the world's problems?

4 Jesus said, 'Countries will fight each other; kingdoms will attack one another. There will be terrible earthquakes, famines and plagues everywhere; there will be strange and terrifying things coming from the sky.' Luke 21:10, 11. Does this mean that political changes, nuclear disarmament, ecology movements and so on are lost causes, and Christians should not waste time campaigning for them?

5 Christians run the risk of going to one of two extremes: either they deal with the world's problems and forget to preach the good news, or they are concerned with people's spiritual needs and forget that we all live in a real, physical world.

Do you think this is true? Which extreme do you think you tend towards? From what you have learnt about Jesus, what do you think his attitude is?

How should we prepare for the future?

6 What do you think is the right attitude for Christians to take regarding the return of Jesus:
- We should study the Bible so that we know when he will return?
- We should live each day as if it were our last?
- We should warn everyone that the end of the world is near?
- We should seek to live as God wants us to live while we have time?
- We should not take any precautions about the future because it may never arrive?
- Or should we combine all of these?

If you are working in a group, discuss these attitudes, and their strengths and weaknesses.

7 From looking at some of the following passages, what do you feel were the three main emphases in what Jesus said about his return? **Luke 21:27, 28; Matthew 25:1-13; Mark 13:26-37;** Matthew 7:21-23; Luke 19:11-27

How will God judge people?

8 How would you answer someone who said, 'How can a God of love punish people?'

Read again pages 183-87 in *Jesus Then and Now*. Do you agree with what the authors have written?

Heavy words about heaven and hell
Jesus spoke very clearly about the judgement of God and about hell as a place of separation from God and his love. Look at Luke 16:19-31; Matthew 18:8-14; Matthew 25:31-46
9 Why did Jesus talk about hell?
10 Why do we find the idea of hell so difficult?
11 What words did Jesus use to describe heaven?
    Read Matthew 13:36-43

What is the Christian hope?

12 We have seen that Jesus talked about the kingdom of God as being here and now. And yet he talks of heaven as 'the kingdom' as well.
     Paul explained to some of the early Christians what it meant to be in the kingdom and yet waiting for the kingdom. You can read what he says: 2 Corinthians 1:21, 22; Ephesians 1:13, 14. Paul also shared how he felt about heaven, in 2 Corinthians 5:1-10.
     Do you ever feel as Paul did?
13 Many of us often have difficulty imagining what heaven will be like. Remember for a few moments some of the times in your life as a Christian when you have experienced God's love and power in a special way. That is a foretaste of what heaven is like! The Bible also gives us some pictures of heaven. Read Revelation 21:1-7; Revelation 21:22 – 22:5; Isaiah 2:4

Thought for action
14 Spend a few moments thinking of ways in which, through the way you live, you can bring the reality of heaven, God's kingdom, into the lives of the people around you each day.

For further reading
The Jesus Hope, Stephen Travis (IVP)
Hereafter, David Winter (Hodder)

NOTES

NOTES

NOTES

NOTES